PRAISE FOR

The 5 Types of Wealth

'I have had a front-row seat to Sahil Bloom's unique journey and have seen his genuine commitment to creating a positive impact with his writing and ideas. This book is a powerful call to action to think deeply about what lights you up – and a guide for how to build a life of meaning and purpose'

TIM COOK, CEO of Apple

'This book is a powerful wake-up call. It will push you to rethink everything about how you're spending your time. It's a compelling call to action that will stay with you long after you've turned the last page'

MEL ROBBINS, *New York Times* bestselling author of *The Let Them Theory* and host of *The Mel Robbins Podcast*

'An important clarifying force in anyone's search to make the best possible choices for their life, and to experience the greatest amount of joy and fulfilment along the way'

ANDREW HUBERMAN, PhD, Stanford professor and host of the *Huberman Lab* podcast

'Sahil Bloom takes us on a deep dive into the science of what matters most in life and how we can cut through life's distractions to stay focused on our real sources of wealth. This book will touch your heart, open your mind and change the way you live'

ROBERT J. WALDINGER, MD, *New York Times* bestselling author of *The Good Life*

'You've always heard that money doesn't buy happiness, but you almost never hear what you should accumulate instead. Sahil Bloom masterfully answers this question. Read this book and start your journey toward the deep satisfaction you want in life'

ARTHUR C. BROOKS, Harvard professor and #1 *New York Times* bestselling author of *From Strength to Strength*

'Great storytelling, great takeaways and great wisdom . . . On almost every page, you'll find yourself discovering ideas that you can't wait to share with the people in your life'

SUSAN CAIN, #1 *New York Times* bestselling author of *Bittersweet* and *Quiet,* and host of the Quiet Life community

'An urgent, emotional gut punch . . . Sahil has a unique ability to weave storytelling, science, history and earned wisdom into a single, clear narrative. It's a must-read for anyone on the journey to fulfilment'

MICHAEL EASTER, *New York Times* bestselling author of *Scarcity Brain*

'Eye-opening and deeply important . . . Sahil Bloom has created a clear, actionable guide to design and build your life around key pillars that bring durable, lasting fulfilment'

GARY VAYNERCHUK, *New York Times* bestselling author of *Twelve and a Half: Leveraging the Emotional Ingredients Necessary for Business Success*

'Sahil Bloom is a master at distilling complex life topics into hard-hitting, actionable insights. This book is a wake-up call to deeply question your priorities and recalibrate around the things that truly matter'

CHRIS WILLIAMSON, host of the *Modern Wisdom* podcast

'*The 5 Types of Wealth* offers a clear, actionable path to define your priorities and build your personal version of a wealthy existence. A must-read!'

ALI ABDAAL, author of *Feel-Good Productivity*

The 5 Types of Wealth Life Planner

ALSO BY SAHIL BLOOM

The 5 Types of Wealth

The 5 Types of Wealth Life Planner

Sahil Bloom

WILLIAM COLLINS

William Collins
An imprint of HarperCollins*Publishers*
1 London Bridge Street
London SE1 9GF

WilliamCollinsBooks.com

HarperCollins*Publishers*
Macken House
39/40 Mayor Street Upper
Dublin 1
D01 C9W8
Ireland

First published in Great Britain in 2025 by William Collins
First published in the United States by Ballantine Books,
an imprint of Random House, a division of Penguin
Random House LLC, New York in 2025

1

Copyright © SBloom Advisory Inc. 2025

Sahil Bloom asserts the moral right to be identified as the author of this work
in accordance with the Copyright, Designs and Patents Act 1988

A catalogue record for this book is available from the British Library

ISBN 978-0-00-880197-7

Brief portions of this work originally appeared on the author's website in different form.

Illustrations by Satvik Dhake

Book design by Caroline Cunningham

All rights reserved. No part of this publication may be reproduced,
stored in a retrieval system, or transmitted, in any form or by
any means, electronic, mechanical, photocopying, recording
or otherwise, without the prior permission of the publishers.

Without limiting the exclusive rights of any author, contributor
or the publisher of this publication, any unauthorised use of this
publication to train generative artificial intelligence (AI) technologies
is expressly prohibited. HarperCollins also exercise their rights under
Article 4(3) of the Digital Single Market Directive 2019/790 and expressly
reserve this publication from the text and data mining exception.

Set in New Caledonia LT Std

Printed and bound in the UK [using 100% renewable electricity at CPI Group (UK) Ltd]

This book contains FSC™ certified paper and other controlled
sources to ensure responsible forest management.

For more information visit: www.harpercollins.co.uk/green

CONTENTS

LETTER TO THE READER	3
Introduction	7
THE 5 TYPES OF WEALTH	9
THE WEALTH SCORE QUIZ	15
The Big Picture	21
THE LIFE RAZOR	23
EXERCISE: CREATE YOUR LIFE RAZOR	26
EXERCISE: CHECKING AND UPDATING YOUR LIFE RAZOR	33
THE LIFE REVIEW	41
THE LIFE REVIEW: REFLECTION QUESTIONS	43
THE LIFE REVIEW: PUTTING IT ALL TOGETHER	61

THE LIFE PLANNING GUIDE	63
GOAL-SETTING FRAMEWORK	65
SYSTEM-BUILDING MENTAL MODELS	71
STRATEGY FOR MONTHLY TRACKING AND ADJUSTING	74
EXERCISE: LIFE PLANNING	75
EXERCISE: MONTHLY TRACKING AND ADJUSTING	85

THE THINK DAY: A QUARTERLY RITUAL THAT WILL CHANGE YOUR LIFE	98

LETTER TO YOUR FUTURE SELF	105

Wealth-Building Exercises 111

TIME WEALTH	113
THE TIME WEALTH HARD RESET	116
THE ENERGY CALENDAR	125
THE TWO-LIST EXERCISE	129
THE EISENHOWER MATRIX	133

SOCIAL WEALTH	138
THE FRONT-ROW PEOPLE VISUALIZATION	141
THE RELATIONSHIP MAP	144

MENTAL WEALTH	**150**
FINDING YOUR *IKIGAI*	152
THE PURSUIT MAP	156
THE 1-1-1 METHOD	163
PHYSICAL WEALTH	**167**
THE EIGHTIETH BIRTHDAY VISUALIZATION	170
THE MORNING ROUTINE	174
FINANCIAL WEALTH	**180**
THE ENOUGH LIFE VISUALIZATION	182
THE 5 TYPES OF WEALTH DECISION TEMPLATE	**187**

Conclusion 189

The 5 Types of Wealth Life Planner

LETTER TO THE READER

"You're going to see your parents fifteen more times before they die."

Those simple words changed my entire life—but only because *I acted on them.*

They were spoken by an old friend who had asked me how I was doing. At the time, I was marching down an all-too-familiar path, chasing money, status, and material things, thinking that they would create a good life. While things were going well on the surface, the deeper realities were showing cracks.

I replied to my friend that it had started to get difficult living so far away from my aging parents, who were on the East Coast, three thousand miles away. I had noticed them slowing down and had grown aware of their mortality for the first time in my life.

He asked how old they were. I said mid-sixties. He asked how often I saw them. I admitted it was down to about once per year. He paused and then spoke those words:

"Okay, so you're going to see your parents fifteen more times before they die."

It was a gut punch. The realization that you have limited time left with the people you care about most can stir emotion in even the most stoic individual.

And in that moment, I was struck by a stark awareness of one fact: My entire definition of success—of what it meant to build a wealthy life—had been incomplete. I was prioritizing one thing—financial success—at the expense of everything else. I was going to win the battle but lose the war.

But awareness is nothing without action.

The next day, my wife and I had a candid conversation about the values we wanted to build our life around. That conversation led to a bold action. Within forty-five days, I had left my job, we had sold our house in California, and we had moved three thousand miles across the country to live closer to both of our sets of parents.

In that dramatic action was a powerful truth: *We were in control.* Of everything. Nobody was coming to save us. We had reassumed agency over our lives.

And if there's one thing I can promise, it's this: You are entirely capable of doing the same. You are entirely capable of squeezing everything you want out of this life. Of doing hard things. Of figuring it out. Of meeting your responsibilities with energy and enthusiasm.

It does not take talent or intelligence, just *courage*.

Throughout your life, you will encounter certain "truths" that are only truths in the sense that they've been repeated so many times that people accept them to be true. It takes courage to question these defaults in a world that profits from your acceptance of them.

The truth is that talent and intelligence are abundant. Courage is not. There's someone out there living the life you want simply because they had the courage to ask the hard questions.

The life you want is on the other side of the questions you dare to ask.

This Life Planner will help you ask those questions and set your life's course. It is designed to be dynamic, iterative, and all-encompassing in its capacity to transform every area of your life. You can and should come back to it regularly for reflection, adjustment, and course correction. The pages that follow will guide you on a journey—a new way to design your life, make better decisions, and take the right actions. The journey is just getting started.

Let's start walking . . .

—Sahil Bloom, New York, November 2025

The people you admire are just the ones who had the courage to start.

The ones who didn't overthink it. The ones who put their ego aside. The ones who walked toward uncertainty. The answer is found in the action.

Introduction

Your wealthy life may be enabled by money, but in the end, it will be defined by everything else.

The 5 Types of Wealth

PYRRHIC VICTORY is a phrase that refers to the victory won at such a steep cost to the victor that it feels like a defeat. The victory damages the victor beyond repair. The battle won, but the war lost.

This is important: A Pyrrhic victory is what you need to avoid in your own life. And unfortunately, a Pyrrhic victory could be where you're headed if you don't change direction.

You're walking this perilous path because of one simple mistake: You're measuring the wrong thing.

Money.

Austrian-born management guru Peter Drucker is often quoted as having said, "What gets measured gets managed." He was right: When a measure of performance becomes an explicit, stated goal, humans will prioritize it, regardless of any associated and unintended consequences. You blind yourself to everything else, focusing on the single measure, no matter the costs elsewhere. Every new promotion, pay raise, and bonus feels like a win as you ignore the painful losses of a war slowly slipping through your fingers.

The war you wage is for happiness, fulfillment, loving relationships, purpose, growth, and health.

If all the battles you're fighting are exclusively about money, you may win these battles, but you will lose the war.

Money is the default life scoreboard, but unfortunately, it's a broken one.

The 5 Types of Wealth is your new life scoreboard:

1. Time Wealth
2. Social Wealth
3. Mental Wealth
4. Physical Wealth
5. Financial Wealth

Each of the five types of wealth is individually important, but it's the relationships across them—the interplay and prioritization—that are critical in building a comprehensively fulfilling existence.

HOW WE'RE TOLD TO MEASURE WEALTH

HOW WE SHOULD

- Social Wealth
- Mental Wealth
- Time Wealth
- Physical Wealth
- Financial Wealth

TIME WEALTH is the freedom to choose how to spend your time, with whom to spend it, where to spend it, and when to trade it for something else. It is characterized by an appreciation and deep understanding of the precious nature of time as an asset—its value and importance. It is the ability to direct deep attention and focus to the highest-leverage activities. It is the control over your time, the ability to establish your own priorities—to set the terms on which you say yes or no to opportunities. If you have a life devoid of Time Wealth, you are trapped in a perpetual loop of busyness, running faster and faster but never making progress, with little control over how time is spent and with whom it is spent.

SOCIAL WEALTH is the connection to others in your personal and professional worlds—the depth and breadth of your connection to those around you. It is the network you can rely on for love and friendship but also for help in times of need. It provides the texture that allows you to appreciate the other types of wealth. What good is the freedom to control your time if you don't have anyone special to spend it with? What joys can physical vitality bring if you can't enjoy physical pursuits with people you love? What satisfaction can money provide if there is no one to dote on? Social Wealth is defined by a few deep, meaningful, healthy relationships and a fulfilling breadth of surface ties throughout your community or culture. If you have a life devoid of Social Wealth, you focus on acquired social status and lack the consequential, weighty relationships that provide lasting satisfaction and joy.

MENTAL WEALTH is the connection to a higher-order purpose and meaning that provides motivation and guides your short- and long-term decision-making. It is grounded in a pursuit of growth that embraces the dynamic potential of your intelligence, ability, and character and an engagement in lifelong learning and development. It is the health of the relationship with the mind, the ability to create space to wrestle with the big, unanswerable questions of life, and the maintenance of rituals that support stillness, balance, clarity, and regeneration. If you have a life devoid of Mental Wealth, you live a life of stasis, self-limiting beliefs, stagnation, low-purpose activities, and perpetual stress.

PHYSICAL WEALTH is your health, fitness, and vitality. Given its grounding in the natural world, it is the most entropic type of wealth, meaning it is more susceptible to natural decay, uncontrollable factors, and blind luck (positive or negative) than other types. Physical Wealth is defined by a focus on the controllable actions around movement, nutrition, and recovery and the creation of consistent habits to promote vigor. If you have a life devoid of Physical Wealth, you lack the discipline to maintain these habits and you are at the mercy of the natural physical deterioration that robs you of enjoyment, particularly in the latter half of life.

FINANCIAL WEALTH is typically defined as financial assets minus financial liabilities, a figure often referred to as *net worth*. On your new scoreboard, there is an added nuance: Your liabilities include your expectations of what you need, your definition of enough. If your expectations rise faster than your assets, you will never have a life of true Financial Wealth, because you'll always need more. Financial Wealth is built upon growing income, managing expenses, and investing the difference in long-term assets that compound meaningfully over time. If you have a life devoid of Financial Wealth, you exist on a treadmill of matching inflows and outflows, a never-ending chase for more.

With these five types of wealth, you have a new scoreboard—a new way to measure your life, because when you measure the right thing, you take the right actions and create the best outcomes.

You can win the battle *and* the war.

Never let the quest for more distract you from the beauty of enough.

The Wealth Score Quiz

Your Wealth Score is your performance on the new scoreboard.

Everyone should take this quiz to establish a baseline Wealth Score prior to continuing with the *Life Planner*. This baseline will be what you measure your progress against as you build and balance your life across the seasons to come. You can and should come back to this assessment in the future to track your progress, just as you might once have tracked your financial net worth using an online tool.

To establish your Wealth Score, you take a simple quiz. There are five statements for each type of wealth; for each statement, respond with 0 (strongly disagree), 1 (disagree), 2 (neutral), 3 (agree), or 4 (strongly agree), then add up your score for each section and the total across the sections.

The maximum score for each type of wealth is 20 (you strongly agree with each of the five statements), and the maximum score overall is 100.

You can take and share a digital version of the Wealth Score Quiz at wealthscorequiz.com.

TIME WEALTH

1. I am in control of my calendar and priorities.
2. I have a deep awareness of the finite, impermanent nature of my time and its importance as my most precious asset.
3. I have a clear understanding of the two to three most important priorities in my personal and professional lives.
4. I am able to consistently direct attention and focus to the important priorities that I have identified.
5. I rarely feel too busy or scattered to spend time on the most important priorities.

SOCIAL WEALTH

1. I have a core set of deep, loving, supportive relationships.
2. I am consistently able to be the partner, parent, family member, and friend that I would want to have.
3. I have a network of loose relationships I can learn from and build on.
4. I have a deep feeling of connection to a community (local, regional, national, spiritual, and so on) or to something bigger than myself.
5. I do not attempt to achieve status, respect, or admiration through material purchases.

MENTAL WEALTH

1. I regularly embrace a childlike curiosity.
2. I have a clear purpose that provides daily meaning and aligns short- and long-term decision-making.
3. I pursue growth and consistently chase my full potential.

4. I have a fundamental belief that I am able to continuously change, develop, and adapt.
5. I have regular rituals that allow me to create space to think, reset, wrestle with questions, and recharge.

PHYSICAL WEALTH

1. I feel strong, healthy, and vital for my age.
2. I move my body regularly through a structured routine and have an active lifestyle.
3. I eat primarily whole, unprocessed foods.
4. I sleep seven or more hours per night on a regular basis and feel rested and recovered.
5. I have a clear plan in place to allow me to physically thrive into my later years.

FINANCIAL WEALTH

1. I have a clear definition of what it means to have enough financially.
2. I have income that is steadily growing alongside my skills and expertise.
3. I manage my monthly expenses so that they are reliably below my income.
4. I have a clear process for investing excess monthly income for long-term compounding.
5. I use my financial wealth as a tool to build other types of wealth.

Using the space provided, log and add up your totals to get your results. Retake the quiz periodically and keep track of your progress.

	Q1	Q2	Q3	Q4	Q5	Total
Time						
Social						
Mental						
Physical						
Financial						

Wealth Score:

Date:

	Q1	Q2	Q3	Q4	Q5	Total
Time						
Social						
Mental						
Physical						
Financial						

Wealth Score:

Date:

	Q1	Q2	Q3	Q4	Q5	Total
Time						
Social						
Mental						
Physical						
Financial						

Wealth Score:

Date:

THE 5 TYPES OF WEALTH LIFE PLANNER

	Q1	Q2	Q3	Q4	Q5	Total
Time						
Social						
Mental						
Physical						
Financial						

Wealth Score:

Date:

	Q1	Q2	Q3	Q4	Q5	Total
Time						
Social						
Mental						
Physical						
Financial						

Wealth Score:

Date:

Using the results from your quiz, fill in the template to get a unique visual perspective on your baseline. The visual will provide a clear understanding of the strengths and weaknesses in your starting point and allow you to create goals to work toward a life of comprehensive wealth.

WEALTH SCORE

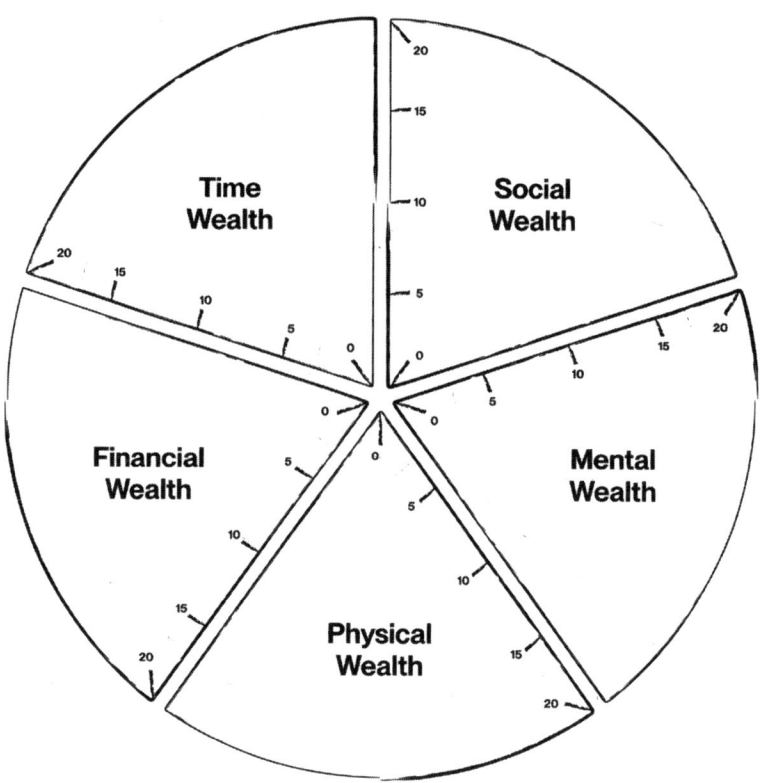

The Big Picture

Surfer Mentality

When a surfer gets up on a wave, they enjoy the present moment, even though they know that the wave will eventually end. They fully enjoy this wave, with the wisdom and awareness that there are always more waves coming.

The Life Razor

IN THE STUDY OF philosophy, the term *razor* denotes any principle that allows you to quickly remove unlikely explanations or avoid unnecessary steps. It allows you to metaphorically shave away unneeded explanations or actions. Today, the term is broadly applied as a rule of thumb that simplifies decision-making.

Inevitably, you will encounter opportunities, chaos, challenges, and complexity that will test you:

- A shiny new job that tempts you to leave the company you love
- The death of a family member or dear friend
- A job loss that takes your financial situation from good to bad
- Health problems that affect those closest to you
- Relationship struggles with someone who once felt like your rock
- A critical decision that feels too heavy and difficult to make

In these moments, you need your own single point of focus—your own rule of thumb to simplify your decision-making.

You need a *Life Razor.*

Your Life Razor is a single statement that will define your presence in the current season of life.

A powerful Life Razor has three core characteristics:

1. Controllable: It should be within your direct control.
2. Ripple-creating: It should have positive second-order effects in other areas of life.
3. Identity-defining: It should be indicative of the type of person you are, the way your ideal self shows up in the world.

Let's walk through an illustrative example of my Life Razor to bring this to life:

"I will coach my son's sports teams."

It is *controllable:* I am in control of making the time to coach my son's sports teams. I can take the actions necessary to have freedom to participate in these activities and to be the type of father he is excited to have around him as a coach.

It is *ripple-creating:* By taking these actions and making this commitment, I will show my son the value I place on our relationship. He will feel empowered by my support. My wife will see my dedication to our son and family and strengthen her dedication to us. My team and business partners will see my family priorities and feel encouraged to establish their own personal priorities, which will make them focused and loyal.

It is *identity-defining:* I am the type of person who coaches my son's sports teams. This person is present, connected to his family and community, committed to his purpose as a father and husband;

he takes care of himself and others and declines opportunities that may infringe upon freedom or jeopardize reputation.

Here's how it might help me navigate a variety of situations in my life:

New professional opportunity: More money and prestige, but more travel and time away for the next two years. I pause and ask myself, "What would the type of person who coaches his son's sports teams do here?" The answer: He would be committed to prioritizing his most important relationships over additional money or prestige. This helps me think through the trade-offs on time and freedom so I can either adjust the opportunity to fit my life or turn it down.

Challenging family situation: It would be easy to ignore or outsource the struggle. I ask myself, "How would the type of person who coaches his son's sports teams step up here?" The answer: He would confront the struggle, face it head-on, and stand as a pillar of strength for his loved ones. This helps me clarify my response and encourage resilience in our family unit.

Life-changing financial opportunity: It carries reputation risk. I might be tempted by the money, but I know that the type of person who coaches his son's sports teams would never jeopardize his son's respect and admiration for money. I pass up the opportunity.

The simple statement "I will coach my son's sports teams" becomes a dynamic defining rule for life: My *Life Razor.*

Now, it's time to define yours.

EXERCISE: CREATE YOUR LIFE RAZOR

"I am the type of person who _____."

The goal is to complete this sentence. To do so, start by listing out the habits, values, and mindsets that embody or capture the way your ideal self shows up in the world.

Habits

_____
_____
_____

Values

_____
_____
_____

Mindsets

_____
_____
_____

What single statement would imply all of the above? What single statement would encapsulate who you are and how your ideal self shows up in the world?

Idea 1: _____

Idea 2: _____

Idea 3: _____

Here are a few illustrative examples from real people who have gone through this exercise that you can use as thought starters.

MID-FORTIES INVESTOR

Habits, Values, and Mindsets: I am disciplined. I delay gratification; I never chase the shiny thing. I wake up early and train my body and mind. I take care of myself and others. I work hard on things that matter to me and take pride in punching the clock for people who are counting on me.

I am the type of person who *wakes up early and does hard things.*

LIFE RAZOR: *I wake up early and do hard things.*

MID-THIRTIES MOTHER

Habits, Values, and Mindsets: I am a caregiver. I am the mother that I wish I had when I was growing up. I always have energy for my kids, no matter how tired I am. I am in a season where I prioritize their growth and development.

I am the type of person who *always tucks my kids into bed.*

LIFE RAZOR: *I always tuck my kids into bed.*

Do Hard Things

Do hard things. Because life is hard. And when you take on voluntary struggle, you're better prepared for the involuntary struggle that inevitably enters your world. Embrace the suck.

MID-TWENTIES CONSULTANT

Habits, Values, and Mindsets: I am fiercely loyal. I am trustworthy. I have high emotional intelligence. I am always there to sit with a friend in need. I prioritize my relationships and the people on the journey with me. I never let someone down if they're counting on me, professionally or personally.

I am the type of person who *never lets a friend cry alone.*

LIFE RAZOR: *I never let a friend cry alone.*

MID-THIRTIES ENTREPRENEUR

Habits, Values, and Mindsets: I prioritize my family and friendships above all else. I show up for the people I love. I am protective, supportive, and giving. I always make it to the game, concert, parent-teacher meeting, or doctor's appointment. I take care of myself physically and mentally so that I can take care of others. I am focused and get things done efficiently to make these priorities work.

I am the type of person who *never misses a recital.*

LIFE RAZOR: *I never miss a recital.*

MID-SIXTIES RETIREE

Habits, Values, and Mindsets: I am a servant leader. I believe in the world-changing power of good deeds. I always take care of others, both in my inner circle and in the extended circles of my community. I value reputation, goodness, and legacy above all near-term pleasures.

I am the type of person who *does one good deed each day (and never tells anyone about it).*

LIFE RAZOR: *I do one good deed each day (and never tell anyone about it).*

Now complete the sentence for yourself:

I am the type of person who _____

_____.

My Life Razor: _____

_____.

Write your Life Razor on a note card or sticky note and place it somewhere visible. It should always be top of mind as you face life's opportunities and challenges. When they come, turn to it.

What would the type of person who _____

_____

do in this situation? How would that person handle it?

Your life will be defined by how you show up at the testing points. Your Life Razor will ensure that you show up as your ideal self.

Courage is not simply one of the virtues, but the form of every virtue at the testing point, which means, at the point of highest reality.

—C. S. Lewis

The Key to Life: Show Up

Show up when it's hard. Show up when it's messy. Show up when no one's watching. Show up when you don't feel like it. Show up when the rewards are uncertain. Just show up. You can never bet against the person who just keeps showing up.

EXERCISE: CHECKING AND UPDATING YOUR LIFE RAZOR

Your Life Razor can (and will) change across the seasons of your life. It may look very different when you're a single twenty-four-year-old from how it does when you're a married forty-year-old—and it will certainly look different when you're a parent to young children, a parent to adult children, or a grandparent.

Revisit the exercise every year to assess its continued value and relevance.

I am the type of person who _____

_____.

My Life Razor: _____

_____.

Does this statement still capture who you are and how your ideal self shows up in the world?

If not, use the pages that follow to update your Life Razor by conducting the original exercise based on the new considerations of your present season of life.

UPDATING YOUR LIFE RAZOR: NEW SEASON 1

Start by listing out the habits, values, and mindsets that embody or capture the way your ideal self shows up in the world.

Habits

_____

_____

_____

Values

_____

_____

_____

Mindsets

_____

_____

_____

What single statement would imply all of the above? What single statement would encapsulate who you are and how your ideal self shows up in the world?

Idea 1: _____

Idea 2: _____

Idea 3: _____

Now complete the sentence for yourself:

I am the type of person who _____

_____.

My Life Razor: _____

_____.

UPDATING YOUR LIFE RAZOR: NEW SEASON 2

Start by listing out the habits, values, and mindsets that embody or capture the way your ideal self shows up in the world.

Habits

_____

_____

_____

Values

_____

_____

_____

Mindsets

_____

_____

_____

What single statement would imply all of the above? What single statement would encapsulate who you are and how your ideal self shows up in the world?

Idea 1: _____

Idea 2: _____

Idea 3: _____

Now complete the sentence for yourself:

I am the type of person who _____

_____.

My Life Razor: _____

_____.

UPDATING YOUR LIFE RAZOR: NEW SEASON 3

Start by listing out the habits, values, and mindsets that embody or capture the way your ideal self shows up in the world.

Habits

_____

_____

_____

Values

_____

_____

_____

Mindsets

_____

_____

_____

What single statement would imply all of the above? What single statement would encapsulate who you are and how your ideal self shows up in the world?

Idea 1: _____

Idea 2: _____

Idea 3: _____

Now complete the sentence for yourself:

I am the type of person who _____

_____.

My Life Razor: _____

_____.

> *We do not learn from experience.... We learn from reflecting on experience.*
>
> —John Dewey

The Life Review

IN OUR RUSH TO look forward, we often forget to look back. This is consequential, because a failure to reflect will eventually result in a failure to grow.

I started conducting a Life Review over ten years ago. It has been a transformative exercise—one that has had an outsized impact on my personal progress and growth.

I trust it will have the same impact for you.

While the Life Review is typically conducted at the end of the calendar year, it is not exclusively confined to that period. The questions it asks and the reflections it prompts are useful throughout the year.

Here are the seven simple questions that may change your life:

It ain't what you don't know that gets you into trouble. It's what you know for sure that just ain't so.

—Mark Twain

QUESTION 1: WHAT DID YOU CHANGE YOUR MIND ON IN THE LAST TWELVE MONTHS?

I USED TO ASSUME that the most successful people in the world had all the answers. That they just knew more than the rest of us. But as I spent more time around these people, I came to realize this was wrong.

The most successful people don't have the right answers—*they ask the right questions.*

They realize that finding the truth is much more important than being right. In fact, they legitimately enjoy being wrong. They lean into the feeling of being an embarrassing beginner. They embrace new information as "software updates" to their brain.

The Life Review starts with that core insight in mind:

- What did you change your mind on in the last twelve months?
- What "software updates" did you have recently?
- What did you know for sure that *just ain't so*?

Remember: If you can't think of anything, that's a bad thing. . . .

EXERCISE: QUESTION 1

What did I change my mind on in the last twelve months?

Personal

_____
_____
_____
_____
_____
_____
_____

Professional

_____
_____
_____
_____
_____
_____
_____

QUESTION 2: WHAT CREATED ENERGY IN THE LAST TWELVE MONTHS?

HERE'S A SIMPLE TRUTH: Outcomes follow energy.

Some things lift you up, make you feel a pull of interest and excitement, while others drag you down, make you feel a drain of exhaustion. When you lean into the opportunities, pursuits, and people that create energy in your life, you achieve the best outcomes.

This question creates awareness of what those specific *energy creators* are in your life, so you can lean into them in the year ahead.

Review your calendars from the last twelve months. Consider the different opportunities, pursuits, and people that occupy space on the calendar. Reflect on how they impacted your energy.

Goal: More time on *energy creators* in the year ahead.

EXERCISE: QUESTION 2

What opportunities, pursuits, or people consistently created energy in my life?

Professional Opportunities

_____
_____
_____
_____

Personal Pursuits

_____
_____
_____
_____

People

_____
_____
_____
_____

Did I spend ample time on these *energy creators,* or did they get neglected?

Professional Opportunities

_____
_____
_____
_____

Personal Pursuits

_____
_____
_____
_____

People

_____
_____
_____
_____

How can I lean into these *energy creators* in the year ahead?

Professional Opportunities

_____
_____
_____
_____

Personal Pursuits

_____
_____
_____
_____

People

_____
_____
_____
_____

QUESTION 3: WHAT DRAINED ENERGY IN THE LAST TWELVE MONTHS?

THERE ARE TWO WAYS to improve your outcomes through energy management:

1. Lean into your *energy creators*
2. Lean away from your *energy drainers*

This question creates awareness of what those specific *energy drainers* are in your life so you can lean away from them in the year ahead.

Continue your review of your calendars from the last twelve months. Consider the different opportunities, pursuits, and people that occupy space on the calendar. Reflect on how they impacted your energy.

Goal: Less time on *energy drainers* in the year ahead.

EXERCISE: QUESTION 3

What opportunities, pursuits, or people consistently drained energy from my life?

Professional Opportunities

_____

_____

Personal Pursuits

People

Did I allow these *energy drainers* to persist, or did I manage them in real time?

Professional Opportunities

Personal Pursuits

People

_____
_____
_____

How can I lean away from these *energy drainers* in the year ahead?

Professional Opportunities

_____
_____
_____
_____

Personal Pursuits

_____
_____
_____
_____

People

_____
_____
_____
_____

QUESTION 4: WHAT ARE THE BOAT ANCHORS IN YOUR LIFE?

BOAT ANCHORS ARE THE people, mindsets, and actions that hold you back from your potential. You're trying to push, full speed ahead, but they create a drag on your life.

Boat anchors can include:

- People who belittle, put down, or diminish your accomplishments. Who laugh at your ambition and tell you to be more realistic. Who harm the quality of your environment through negativity and pessimism.
- Self-limiting beliefs, stories, and mindsets.
- Bad habits that cut into your growth.

This question asks you to identify the boat anchors that exist in your life.

Goal: Eliminate or minimize them in the year ahead.

EXERCISE: QUESTION 4

What are the boat anchors in my life?

People

_____
_____
_____
_____

Beliefs, Stories, and Mindsets

_____
_____
_____
_____

Habits

_____
_____
_____
_____

We suffer more in imagination than in reality.

—S͟ENECA

Fear Comes from Inexperience, Not Incapability

You're afraid because you haven't done it yet, not because you can't do it. Inexperience is the problem to be solved—and it's solved through having the courage to act.

QUESTION 5: WHAT ARE YOU NOT DOING BECAUSE OF FEAR?

ONE THING I'VE LEARNED: Sometimes you don't give your best effort because you're afraid of what will happen if you do give it your all and still fail.

But that *self-protection* can quickly become *self-rejection*.

The thing you fear the most is often the thing you most need to do.

This question forces you to deconstruct your fear:

- What was the downside if you had taken action?
- What was the upside if you had taken action?

Goal: Get closer to your fears in the year ahead.

EXERCISE: QUESTION 5

What am I not doing because of fear?

FEAR 1:
_____

Downsides from Action
_____
_____

Upsides from Action

_____

_____

FEAR 2:

_____

Downsides from Action

_____

_____

Upsides from Action

_____

_____

FEAR 3:

_____

Downsides from Action

_____

_____

Upsides from Action

_____

_____

QUESTION 6: WHAT WERE YOUR GREATEST HITS AND WORST MISSES IN THE LAST TWELVE MONTHS?

YOUR NATURAL BIAS SKEWS how you see your life:

- The optimist sees all hits.
- The pessimist sees all misses.

This question's objective is to take a balanced view: Write down your hits and your misses. Reflect on why the hits hit and the misses missed.

EXERCISE: QUESTION 6

What were my greatest hits and worst misses in the last twelve months?

Greatest Hits

_____
_____
_____
_____
_____
_____

Reflection: Why did the hits hit?

_____
_____
_____
_____
_____
_____
_____

Worst Misses

_____
_____
_____
_____
_____
_____
_____

Reflection: Why did the misses miss?

_____
_____
_____
_____
_____
_____
_____

QUESTION 7: WHAT DID YOU LEARN IN THE LAST TWELVE MONTHS?

IT'S EASY TO LOSE sight of your progress and growth when you're zoomed in. This question pushes you to zoom out and reclaim your perspective.

Take your time on this one. Reflect on the other questions from the exercise. Write down what you've learned.

EXERCISE: QUESTION 7

What did I learn in the last twelve months?

_____
_____
_____
_____
_____
_____
_____
_____
_____
_____
_____
_____
_____
_____
_____
_____
_____

When you stop learning, you start dying.

—Albert Einstein

THE LIFE REVIEW: PUTTING IT ALL TOGETHER

The Seven-Question Life Review:

1. What did I change my mind on in the last twelve months?
2. What created energy in the last twelve months?
3. What drained energy in the last twelve months?
4. What are the boat anchors in my life?
5. What am I not doing because of fear?
6. What were my greatest hits and worst misses in the last twelve months?
7. What did I learn in the last twelve months?

To get even more out of it, try conducting the Life Review in a small-group format.

Go through the questions individually, then get together with a small group and walk through your reflection and responses.

Pressure test. Question assumptions. Provide feedback. Create accountability.

The Life Review is a life-changing exercise. Wrestle with the questions, use the insights to set your course, and then take action to spark growth in the year ahead.

Nobody Is Thinking About You

You aren't afraid of failure. You're afraid of what other people will think of you if you fail. Well, no one is thinking about you. They're too busy thinking about themselves. So go do the damn thing.

The Life Planning Guide

On my thirty-second birthday, my parents gave me a small silver compass inscribed with a short message: "So you may always know where your true north lies."

The deeper message was clear:

> *Life is about direction, not speed. It's much better to climb slowly up the right mountain than it is to climb fast up the wrong one.*

This Life Planning process is your *compass:* setting your direction for the years ahead and establishing a regular cadence of check-ins to maintain your adaptability on the journey.

This compass works synergistically with your Life Razor: Your Life Razor establishes your identity—who you are and what you stand for—while your compass defines where you're going, your vision for the future. You will turn to your Life Razor when challenges or opportunities arise, but your compass will dictate your direction as you build toward your dream life.

The Life Planning Guide will equip you with the structure you need to set your course for a bright future in the years ahead.

GOAL-SETTING FRAMEWORK

THE GOAL-SETTING FRAMEWORK HAS four connected components:

1. Big Goals
2. Checkpoint Goals
3. Daily Systems
4. Anti-Goals

Here's how it works, with an illustrative example of each to bring it to life:

BIG GOALS

These are your big, long-term goals. They should be large and ambitious. If these Big Goals don't scare you a little bit, I'd encourage you to think bigger.

The Big Goals are the summit of the mountain—motivating on a macro scale, but too far off and intimidating to be motivating on a micro, daily basis.

Big Goal Illustrative Example: Create a movement of ten million people around the world who have read *The 5 Types of Wealth* and taken actions to build their lives around the priorities that matter to them.

CHECKPOINT GOALS

Work backward from your Big Goals to formulate a set of Checkpoint Goals.

If the Big Goals are the summit of the mountain, the Checkpoint Goals are the mid-climb campsites. You can't reach the summit without reaching these points, as all paths lead directly through them.

Checkpoint Goal Illustrative Example: Sell one million copies within the first eighteen months of launch.

DAILY SYSTEMS

These are the two or three daily actions that you need to take to create tangible, compounding forward progress. The simplest daily actions to generate progress in each arena.

If the Big Goals and Checkpoint Goals are your compass, establishing your direction, the Daily Systems are your feet, moving you forward on your climb.

Daily Systems Illustrative Example: Movements are built through unscalable actions. Interacting with readers one-on-one is a key part of creating evangelists for the message. Spend thirty minutes daily engaging with readers. Content creation is at the core of attracting new eyes to the message. Sixty minutes of daily reading, sixty minutes of daily thinking, and sixty minutes of daily creation will keep everything moving forward.

You don't plan your future. You plan your actions today, and those actions create your future.

ANTI-GOALS

Anti-Goals are the things we don't want to happen on our journey to achieve our Big Goals.

If the Big Goals are your summit, Anti-Goals are the things you don't want to sacrifice while executing the climb—like your life, your toes, or your sanity. You want to reach the summit, but not at the expense of these things.

For example, your Big Goal might be to become CEO of your company, but your Anti-Goals might be spending over two hundred nights away from your family and allowing your health to suffer from constant travel and stress. You want to achieve the Big Goal, but not if it means having those Anti-Goals become real.

Anti-Goals are guardrails—they allow you to win the battle *and* the war.

Anti-Goal Illustrative Example: Traveling for more than ten nights out of the month (I don't want to miss this precious time with my wife and son), sacrificing my health and family are nonnegotiables to achieve the Big Goal.

All I want to know is where I'm going to die, so I'll never go there.

—Charlie Munger

Your Entire Life Will Change When You Realize That Anything Above Zero Compounds.

Showing up consistently matters more than showing up perfectly. Small things become big things. Never allow optimal to get in the way of beneficial.

SYSTEM-BUILDING MENTAL MODELS

HARSH TRUTH: IDEAS ARE cheap; execution is expensive.

Even with our Big Goals to motivate us and our Daily Systems all planned out, we may fail to execute. To guide your execution against your Daily Systems, here are three system-building mental models to support you on your journey:

THE ABC SYSTEM (SAHIL'S FAVORITE)

Establish three levels for every Daily System:

- A: Most ambitious, perfect case
- B: Middle ground, base case
- C: Minimum viable level

On days when you feel great, you hit your A level. On days when you feel okay, you hit your B level. On days when you feel bad, just hit your C level.

The ABC System removes any intimidation or guilt: If you hit your C, you're making forward progress.

Anything above zero compounds.

The system prevents optimal (A) from getting in the way of beneficial (C) and gives you the flexibility to make progress while allowing the inevitable chaos of life to enter.

THE TWO-DAY RULE

With whatever habit you're trying to build, never allow yourself to skip more than one day in a row.

A study in the *European Journal of Social Psychology* found, "Missing one opportunity to perform the behavior did not materially affect the habit formation process."[*]

In other words, skipping one day won't hurt your habit building, as long as you don't skip the next one.

Never skip twice.

THE 30-FOR-30 APPROACH

In any arena in which you want to make progress, do the thing for thirty minutes per day for thirty straight days.

This approach works for three reasons:

1. Thirty days of effort is a real commitment. If you're half in, you won't want to take it on and commit to the thirty days.
2. Thirty minutes per day is short enough that you can mentally take it on. Pre-start self-intimidation is one of the biggest drivers of stagnation.
3. Thirty days of thirty minutes per day is nine hundred total minutes of accumulated effort. This will yield surprisingly significant results.

30-for-30 creates a marathon of short, manageable sprints.

---

[*] Source: Phillippa Lally et al., "How Are Habits Formed: Modelling Habit Formation in the Real World," *European Journal of Social Psychology* 40, no. 6 (2010): 998–1009, https://onlinelibrary.wiley.com/doi/abs/10.1002/ejsp.674.

The Most Dangerous Person in the World

is the one who shows up every single day even when the rewards are uncertain. The one who can tolerate the most uncertainty is the one who will eventually win.

STRATEGY FOR MONTHLY TRACKING AND ADJUSTING

THERE'S A CONCEPT IN aviation called the *1-in-60 Rule*, which says that a one-degree error in heading will cause a plane to miss its target by one mile for every sixty miles flown. Tiny deviations from the optimal course are amplified by distance and time. A small miss now creates a very large miss later.

The concept applies directly to your Life Planning and highlights the importance of real-time course corrections and adjustments.

Conduct a three-question monthly check-in on the last Friday of each month:

1. What really matters in your life right now, and are your Big Goals still aligned with this? Assess the quality of your goals and ensure that they still feel appropriate.
2. Are your current Daily Systems aligned with your Big Goals? Assess the quality of your Daily Systems and whether they are creating the appropriate momentum.
3. Are you in danger of running afoul of your Anti-Goals? Assess the quality of your environment and decisions to evaluate any changes that need to be made.

The ritual takes about thirty minutes each month and creates an opportunity for regular reflection and minor course corrections that are essential on your journey.

EXERCISE: LIFE PLANNING

Use the space on the pages that follow to conduct your Life Planning process.

STEP 1: DETERMINE CORE FOCUS AREAS

An old school of thought would contend that your focus on each type of wealth exists in a binary state: on or off. It would say that you can have, at most, two types flipped on at any point in time and that the other three types would have to be flipped off.

This book rejects that old school of thought and offers a new one: Each area of your life exists on a *dimmer switch*. You will have one or two areas that are your primary focus during the present season (the dimmer switch turned up) and three or four areas that are not the focus (the dimmer switch turned down low).

To begin your Life Planning process, you must first establish those focus areas.

Review your current Wealth Score, life responsibilities, and considerations.

What are my primary focus areas for the present season of life? (Choose one or two.)

- ☐ Time Wealth
- ☐ Social Wealth
- ☐ Mental Wealth
- ☐ Physical Wealth
- ☐ Financial Wealth

STEP 2: ESTABLISH BIG GOALS

My primary focus areas for the present season of life are _____ and _____.

WHAT ARE MY ONE TO THREE BIG GOALS ASSOCIATED WITH EACH FOCUS AREA?

Focus Area 1: _____

Big Goal 1: _____
Why is this important? _____
_____

Big Goal 2: _____
Why is this important? _____
_____

Big Goal 3: _____
Why is this important? _____
_____

Focus Area 2: _____

Big Goal 1: _____
*Why is this important?*_____
_____

Big Goal 2: _____
Why is this important? _____
_____

Big Goal 3: _____
Why is this important? _____
_____

STEP 3: ESTABLISH ASSOCIATED CHECKPOINT GOALS

My first primary focus area for the present season of life is _____.

MY BIG GOALS FOR THIS FOCUS AREA ARE:

Big Goal 1: _____
Big Goal 2: _____
Big Goal 3: _____

WHAT ARE MY CHECKPOINT GOALS FOR EACH BIG GOAL?

Checkpoint Goal (Big Goal 1): _____
Checkpoint Goal (Big Goal 2): _____
Checkpoint Goal (Big Goal 3): _____

My second primary focus area for the present season of life is _____.

MY BIG GOALS FOR THIS FOCUS AREA ARE:

Big Goal 1: _____
Big Goal 2: _____
Big Goal 3: _____

WHAT ARE MY CHECKPOINT GOALS FOR EACH BIG GOAL?

    Checkpoint Goal (Big Goal 1): _____
    Checkpoint Goal (Big Goal 2): _____
    Checkpoint Goal (Big Goal 3): _____

STEP 4: ESTABLISH SPECIFIC DAILY SYSTEMS

WHAT ARE MY DAILY SYSTEMS TO PROGRESS TOWARD EACH CHECKPOINT GOAL?

    Focus Area 1: _____

        Big Goal 1: _____
        Checkpoint Goal: _____

        Daily System 1: _____
        Daily System 2: _____
        Daily System 3: _____

        Big Goal 2: _____
        Checkpoint Goal: _____

        Daily System 1: _____
        Daily System 2: _____
        Daily System 3: _____

        Big Goal 3: _____
        Checkpoint Goal: _____

Daily System 1: _____
Daily System 2: _____
Daily System 3: _____

Focus Area 2: _____

Big Goal 1: _____
Checkpoint Goal: _____

Daily System 1: _____
Daily System 2: _____
Daily System 3: _____

Big Goal 2: _____
Checkpoint Goal: _____

Daily System 1: _____
Daily System 2: _____
Daily System 3: _____

Big Goal 3: _____
Checkpoint Goal: _____

Daily System 1: _____
Daily System 2: _____
Daily System 3: _____

STEP 5: ESTABLISH ANTI-GOALS

Three questions to inform your creation of Anti-Goals:

- What are the worst possible outcomes that could occur from your pursuit of these Big Goals?
- What could lead to that worst possible outcome occurring?
- What would you view as winning the battle but losing the war?

Responses

_____

_____

_____

Anti-Goal 1: _____

Anti-Goal 2: _____

Anti-Goal 3: _____

STEP 6: ESTABLISH LOW-DIMMER SYSTEMS

With your goals and systems for the primary focus areas established, spend a few minutes creating the low-intensity Daily Systems for the non-focus areas (where the dimmer switch is turned down low).

Illustrative Example 1: If Social Wealth is not the primary focus, I can still establish a Daily System to send a text to one friend each day to let them know I'm thinking about them. Low time-intensity but maintains these bonds. A small daily action that promotes progress and prevents atrophy.

Illustrative Example 2: If Physical Wealth is not the primary focus, I can still establish a Daily System to go for a thirty-minute walk every day. Low time-intensity but maintains a level of fitness and health from basic daily movement. A small daily action that promotes progress and prevents atrophy.

For ideas on high-leverage Daily Systems that will allow you to maintain and progress with the dimmer turned down low, see the guide chapters at the end of each major section in The 5 Types of Wealth.

What are my non-focus areas for the present season of life?

- ☐ Time Wealth
- ☐ Social Wealth
- ☐ Mental Wealth
- ☐ Physical Wealth
- ☐ Financial Wealth

WHAT IS ONE LOW-INTENSITY DAILY SYSTEM FOR EACH NON-FOCUS AREA THAT WILL CONTRIBUTE TO ITS MAINTENANCE OR FORWARD PROGRESS?

Non-Focus Area 1: _____

Low-Dimmer Daily System: _____

Non-Focus Area 2: _____

Low-Dimmer Daily System: _____

Non-Focus Area 3: _____

Low-Dimmer Daily System: _____

LIFE PLANNING PROCESS: PUTTING IT ALL TOGETHER

Focus Area 1: _____

   Big Goal 1: _____
   _____
   _____

   Checkpoint Goal: _____
   _____
   _____

   Daily Systems: _____

   Big Goal 2: _____
   _____
   _____

   Checkpoint Goal: _____
   _____
   _____

   Daily Systems: _____

   Big Goal 3: _____
   _____
   _____

   Checkpoint Goal: _____
   _____
   _____

   Daily Systems: _____

Anti-Goals: _____

THE 5 TYPES OF WEALTH LIFE PLANNER

Focus Area 2: _____

   Big Goal 1: _____
   _____
   _____

   Checkpoint Goal: _____
   _____
   _____

   Daily Systems: _____

   Big Goal 2: _____
   _____
   _____

   Checkpoint Goal: _____
   _____
   _____

   Daily Systems: _____

   Big Goal 3: _____
   _____
   _____

   Checkpoint Goal: _____
   _____
   _____

   Daily Systems: _____

Anti-Goals: _____

Non-Focus Areas: _____

Low-Dimmer System 1: _____

_____

_____

Low-Dimmer System 2: _____

_____

_____

Low-Dimmer System 3: _____

_____

_____

EXERCISE: MONTHLY TRACKING AND ADJUSTING

Use the space on the pages that follow to conduct your three-question monthly check-in.

MONTH 1

What really matters in my life right now, and are my Big Goals still aligned with this?

_____
_____
_____

Are my current Daily Systems aligned with my Big Goals?

_____
_____
_____

Am I in danger of running afoul of my Anti-Goals?

_____
_____
_____

Based on the reflections above, what (if any) adjustments are necessary to stay on course?

_____
_____
_____

MONTH 2

What really matters in my life right now, and are my Big Goals still aligned with this?

_____
_____
_____

Are my current Daily Systems aligned with my Big Goals?

_____
_____
_____

Am I in danger of running afoul of my Anti-Goals?

_____
_____
_____

Based on the reflections above, what (if any) adjustments are necessary to stay on course?

_____
_____
_____

MONTH 3

What really matters in my life right now, and are my Big Goals still aligned with this?

_____
_____
_____

Are my current Daily Systems aligned with my Big Goals?

_____
_____
_____

Am I in danger of running afoul of my Anti-Goals?

_____
_____
_____

Based on the reflections above, what (if any) adjustments are necessary to stay on course?

_____
_____
_____

MONTH 4

What really matters in my life right now, and are my Big Goals still aligned with this?

_____
_____
_____

Are my current Daily Systems aligned with my Big Goals?

_____
_____
_____

Am I in danger of running afoul of my Anti-Goals?

_____
_____
_____

Based on the reflections above, what (if any) adjustments are necessary to stay on course?

_____
_____
_____

MONTH 5

What really matters in my life right now, and are my Big Goals still aligned with this?

_____
_____
_____

Are my current Daily Systems aligned with my Big Goals?

_____
_____
_____

Am I in danger of running afoul of my Anti-Goals?

_____
_____
_____

Based on the reflections above, what (if any) adjustments are necessary to stay on course?

_____
_____
_____

MONTH 6

What really matters in my life right now, and are my Big Goals still aligned with this?

_____
_____
_____

Are my current Daily Systems aligned with my Big Goals?

_____
_____
_____

Am I in danger of running afoul of my Anti-Goals?

_____
_____
_____

Based on the reflections above, what (if any) adjustments are necessary to stay on course?

_____
_____
_____

MONTH 7

What really matters in my life right now, and are my Big Goals still aligned with this?

_____
_____
_____

Are my current Daily Systems aligned with my Big Goals?

_____
_____
_____

Am I in danger of running afoul of my Anti-Goals?

_____
_____
_____

Based on the reflections above, what (if any) adjustments are necessary to stay on course?

_____
_____
_____

MONTH 8

What really matters in my life right now, and are my Big Goals still aligned with this?

_____
_____
_____

Are my current Daily Systems aligned with my Big Goals?

_____
_____
_____

Am I in danger of running afoul of my Anti-Goals?

_____
_____
_____

Based on the reflections above, what (if any) adjustments are necessary to stay on course?

_____
_____
_____

MONTH 9

What really matters in my life right now, and are my Big Goals still aligned with this?

_____
_____
_____

Are my current Daily Systems aligned with my Big Goals?

_____
_____
_____

Am I in danger of running afoul of my Anti-Goals?

_____
_____
_____

Based on the reflections above, what (if any) adjustments are necessary to stay on course?

_____
_____
_____

MONTH 10

What really matters in my life right now, and are my Big Goals still aligned with this?

_____
_____
_____

Are my current Daily Systems aligned with my Big Goals?

_____
_____
_____

Am I in danger of running afoul of my Anti-Goals?

_____
_____
_____

Based on the reflections above, what (if any) adjustments are necessary to stay on course?

_____
_____
_____

MONTH 11

What really matters in my life right now, and are my Big Goals still aligned with this?

_____
_____
_____

Are my current Daily Systems aligned with my Big Goals?

_____
_____
_____

Am I in danger of running afoul of my Anti-Goals?

_____
_____
_____

Based on the reflections above, what (if any) adjustments are necessary to stay on course?

_____
_____
_____

MONTH 12

What really matters in my life right now, and are my Big Goals still aligned with this?

_____
_____
_____

Are my current Daily Systems aligned with my Big Goals?

_____
_____
_____

Am I in danger of running afoul of my Anti-Goals?

_____
_____
_____

Based on the reflections above, what (if any) adjustments are necessary to stay on course?

_____
_____
_____

The greatest discoveries in life come not from finding the right answers but from asking the right questions.

The Think Day: A Quarterly Ritual That Will Change Your Life

THE CONCEPT OF A Think Day is a more actionable adaptation of the *Think Week* practice first popularized by Bill Gates in the 1980s. Gates would seclude himself in a remote location, shut off communication, and spend a week reading and thinking. It allowed him to exit the demands of an average day on the job and zoom out to see the bigger picture.

The Think Day is a quarterly ritual to create space, reclaim perspective, and wrestle with the bigger-picture questions about your life.

Pick one day at the end of the quarter and plan one to two hours to step out of your day-to-day demands:

- Separate yourself from your normal environments (mentally or physically). Ideally, you'd place yourself in an inspiring space, such as a house in nature or a big, open coffee shop.
- Bring a journal, pen, and open mind. No fancy tools or devices required.
- Shut off all your devices. This forces you to shut off the constant stimulus drip. This is important.

The goal is to zoom out, open your mind, and think creatively—about your direction, vision, goals, and values.

Here are four big-picture questions to think and reflect on:

If you were the main character in a movie of your life, what would the audience be screaming at you to do right now?

___

___

___

We've all been there: watching a movie and the main character is clearly veering off course. We feel that urge to scream at them:

- Look out behind you!
- Chase her to the airport!
- Don't go down in that basement!

You are that main character in the movie of your life—and the audience would be screaming something at you right now. So, what is it? What is blindingly obvious from the outside looking in that you are choosing to ignore or have yet to create enough perspective to see?

___

___

___

Perspective is everything. Ask this question to detach yourself from your situation and see it through someone else's eyes.

If someone observed your actions for a week, what would they say your priorities are?

_____
_____
_____
_____
_____
_____
_____

How serious would the observer say you are about your goals?

_____
_____
_____
_____
_____
_____
_____

There are two types of priorities in life:

1. The priorities you say you have
2. The priorities your actions show you have

For many of us, there is a significant gap between the two. The goal is to identify the gap and adjust our actions to close it.

If you repeated your current typical day for one hundred days, would your life be better or worse?

_____
_____
_____

The zoomed-in perspective makes it difficult to assess the quality of your daily actions. This question forces you to zoom out:

- How would your actions from a typical day compound in your life?

  _____
  _____
  _____
  _____

- Would they be driving you forward in the direction of your goals and vision?

  _____
  _____
  _____
  _____

- Would they be steering you off course?

  _____
  _____
  _____
  _____

Course correct early and often.

Are you hunting antelope or field mice?

A lion is fully capable of capturing, killing, and eating a field mouse. But it turns out that the energy required to do so exceeds the caloric content of the mouse itself. So a lion that spent its day hunting and eating field mice would slowly starve to death. A lion can't live on field mice. A lion needs antelope. Antelope are big animals. They take more speed and strength to capture and kill, and once killed, they provide a feast for the lion and her pride. A lion can live a long and happy life on a diet of antelope. The distinction is important.*

Think of antelope as the big, important problems, while field mice are the tiny, urgent ones.

Are you focusing on the big, important tasks that provide sufficient reward for your energy? Or are you too busy chasing tiny wins that won't move the needle?

_____
_____
_____
_____
_____
_____
_____

Always strive to hunt antelope!

* Source: James Carville and Paul Begala, *Buck Up, Suck Up . . . and Come Back When You Foul Up: 12 Winning Secrets from the War Room* (New York: Simon & Schuster, 2003).

Live the questions. Someday, without even realizing it, you will live your way into the answers.

—Rainer Maria Rilke,
Letters to a Young Poet

There is no favorable wind for the sailor who doesn't know where to go.

—S<small>ENECA</small>

Letter to Your Future Self

On January 1, 2014, as I was graduating from college, I wrote a letter to my future self. I sealed the letter in an envelope that read *Open on January 1, 2024*, and placed it in my small personal safe.

Ten years later, on January 1, 2024, as I was about to turn in the final draft of *The 5 Types of Wealth*, I opened the letter and was knocked off my feet.

As I reread the letter, one conclusion screamed off the page:

The answers are within you—you just haven't found the right questions yet.

January 1, 2014

Hey Old Man –

If you're reading this, it means you're alive, so congrats on that, I guess.

I'm about to graduate and enter the *real world*, whatever that means, so it feels like an appropriate moment to lay out some hopes for my future:

1. I hope you married Elizabeth. Seriously, I hope you didn't fuck that up. She's the best thing that ever happened to you.

2. I hope you've got a kid by now. I don't want kids, but I imagine I might grow up at some point and change my mind on that. If you do have kids, I hope you're a good dad. If you're even half as good as your dad was to you, you'll be great.

3. I really hope you've worked on yourself and grown up. You have a lot you hide from the world. You're insecure. You compare yourself to everyone but yourself. You're so afraid to fail that you always seem to choose the safe path. You've got work to do—don't run away from it.

4. I hope you tell your parents you love them more often. They don't know how much they mean to you, and that's a shame.

5. I hope you live closer to your family. You made your mom really sad when you took that job in California. She smiled and said she was happy for you, but it was that sad smile that her parents gave her when she left for college in America. The smile of losing a child to a new world. Don't let that be the case.

6. I hope you got closer to Sonali. Sibling love is special, but you've allowed your competitiveness to get in the way of that at times. I hope you've gotten past that and embraced each other in a new light. You can learn a lot from her.

7. I hope you're working on something that feels meaningful. I don't even know what that means, to be honest, but I guess it's something like enjoying a random Tuesday.

8. I hope the friends you love and care about are all healthy and thriving. I know that's probably impossible, so I guess I hope the friends you love and care about knows you love and care about them. That's all that matters in the end.

9. And finally, I hope you've had a little bit of fun along the way.

That's all for now. I don't know how you sign off a letter like this. Goodbye for now, I guess.

Sahil

On the pages that follow, write a letter to your future self one year from now. If you don't know where to begin, start with these prompts:

- What are your hopes for the future?
- What will you be celebrating on that future date when you open the letter?
- What are the things you know that you need to remove from your life?
- What do you believe you are meant for that the future will reveal to be true?
- What are your greatest fears?

Reflect on *where you are* and *where you hope to be* when you open the letter. Vividly imagine that desired future.

DATE TODAY: _____

DATE TO OPEN: _____

_____
_____
_____
_____
_____
_____
_____
_____
_____
_____

This letter is your *true north*—it will set your direction; the answers you already have within you. This imagined future is yours to create. It's time to start asking the right questions to turn this imagined future into reality.

Get Your Dopamine from Action

Dopamine from information gathering is a dangerous drug.
Your entire life will change the moment you stop looking for more
information and start acting on the information you already have.

Wealth-Building Exercises

With the bigger-picture vision and plan in alignment, the sections that follow will guide you through a series of valuable, high-leverage exercises to build each type of wealth into your life.

Time Wealth

TIME WEALTH IS BUILT upon three core pillars:

- *Awareness:* An understanding of the finite, impermanent nature of time
- *Attention:* The ability to direct your attention and focus on the things that matter (and ignore the rest)
- *Control:* The freedom to own your time and choose exactly how to spend it

In this section, you'll be guided through four exercises to build Time Wealth:

1. The Time Wealth Hard Reset
2. The Energy Calendar
3. The Two-List Exercise
4. The Eisenhower Matrix

These systems are supported by clear research and battle-tested through my own personal experience. This isn't one-size-fits-all, and you shouldn't feel compelled to complete every single one; browse through and select those that feel most relevant and useful to you.

How many moments do you really have remaining with your loved ones? It's probably not as many as you'd like to believe. All the tiny moments, people, and experiences that we take for granted will eventually be ones we wish we had more of.

THE TIME WEALTH HARD RESET

In November 2022, I came across data from the American Time Use Survey on who we spend our time with over the course of our lives. The insights are simultaneously depressing and inspiring.

Here are the six graphs of the data that everyone needs to see:

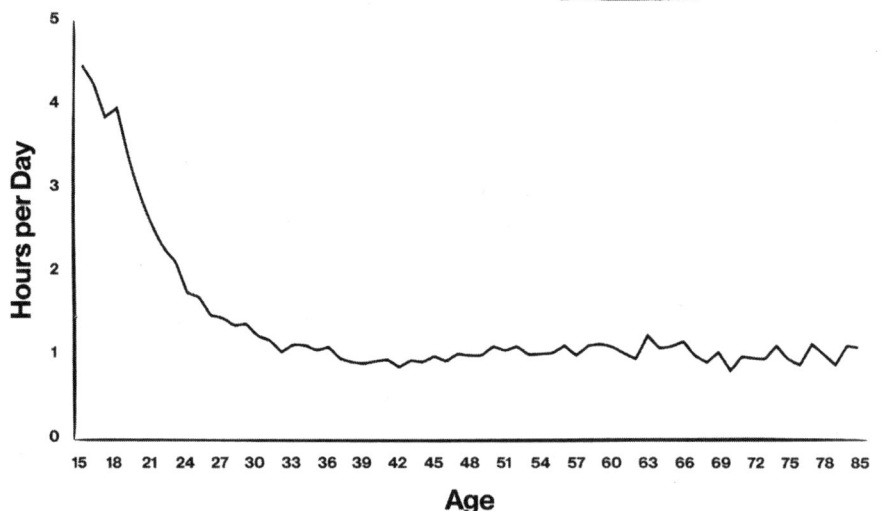

Time spent with your parents and siblings peaks in childhood and declines sharply after you reach age twenty. As you leave home and get caught up in your own life, you often fail to recognize that the time you have remaining with your family is so very limited. Cherish these relationships while you can.

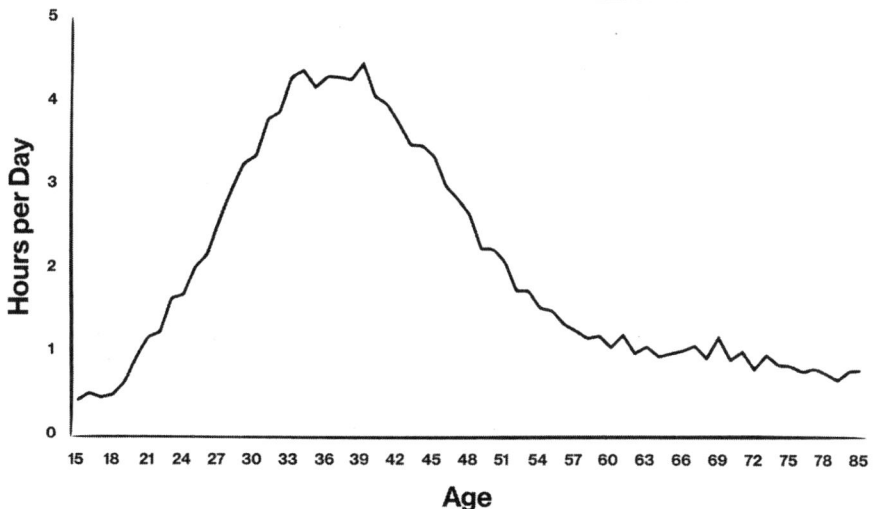

Time spent with your children peaks in the early years of their life and declines sharply thereafter. There's a devastatingly short window during which you are your child's entire world. Don't blink and miss it.

TIME SPENT WITH FRIENDS

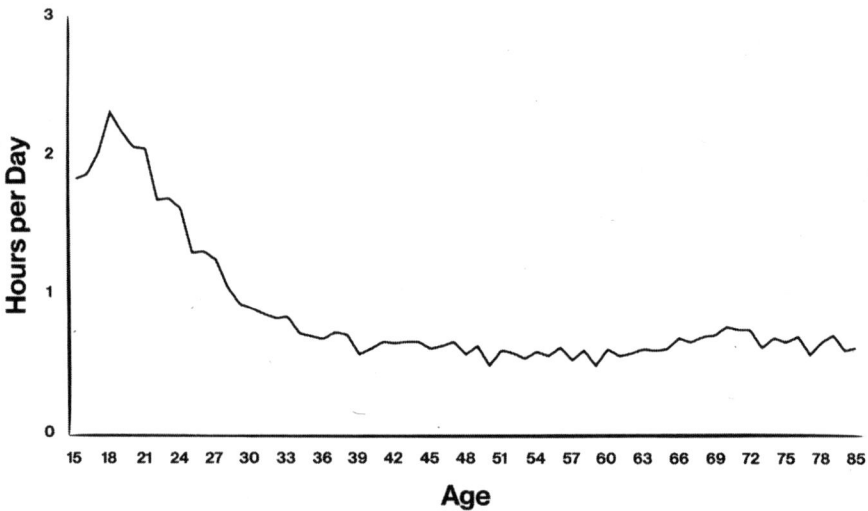

Time spent with your friends peaks when you're eighteen and then declines sharply to a low baseline. In your youth, you spend a lot of time with a lot of friends. As you enter adulthood, you spend a little bit of time with a few close friends. Embrace the breadth of friendships that comes with youth, and prioritize the depth of friendships that should come with age.

TIME SPENT WITH PARTNER

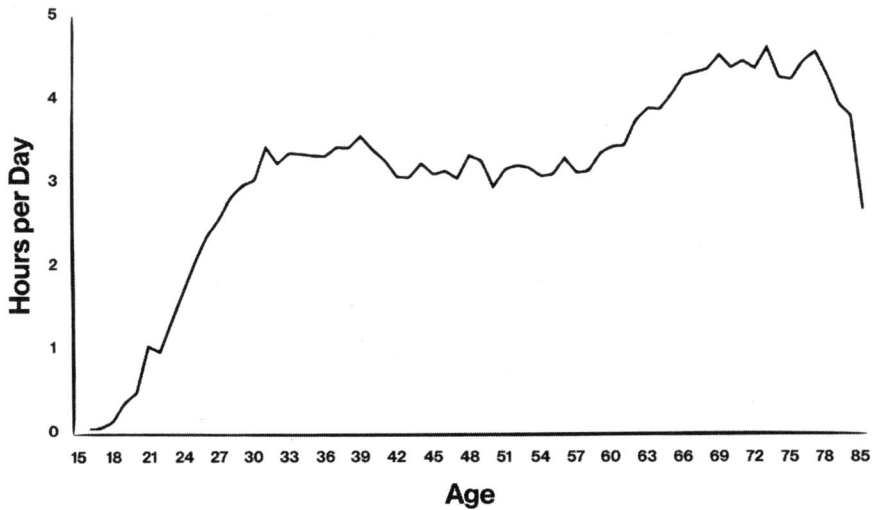

Time spent with your partner trends up until death. The person you choose to confront life's ups and downs with will have the largest impact on your happiness and fulfillment. Choose wisely.

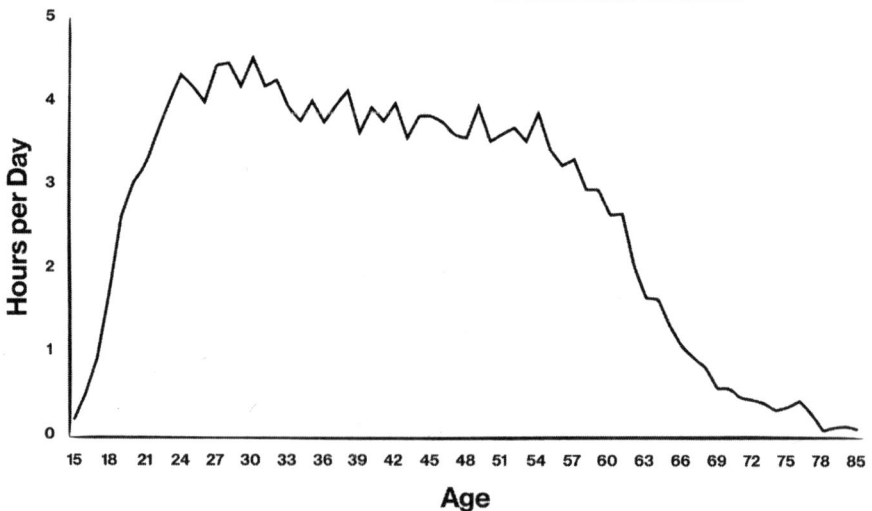

Time spent with coworkers is steady during the traditional prime working years, from age twenty to age sixty, and declines sharply thereafter. Work will pull you away from your family and loved ones throughout your life. If you have the luxury of choice, make sure you choose work—and coworkers—that you find meaningful and important. Aim to have coworkers who create energy in your life.

TIME SPENT ALONE

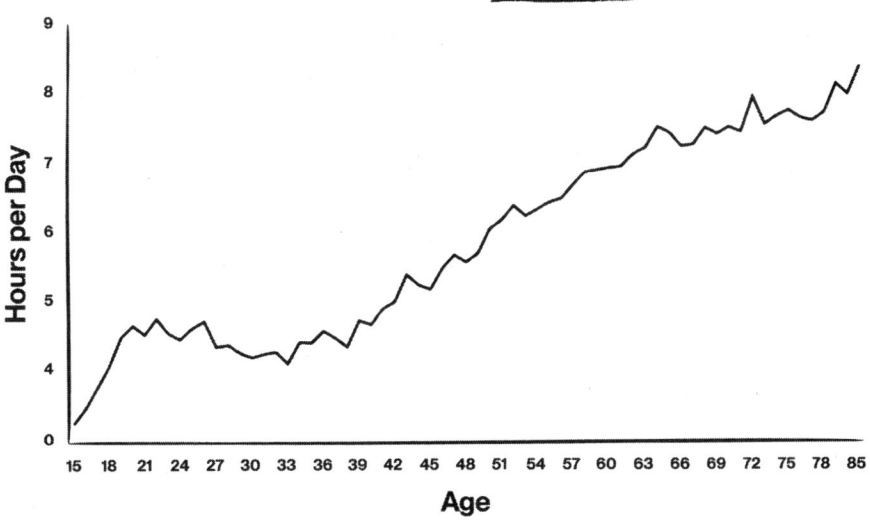

Time spent alone steadily increases throughout your life. When you're young, you tend to view time alone as a sign of not fitting in. You come to fear time alone, to fear boredom. But you need to learn to cherish it. Find happiness and joy in the time you have to yourself—there will be more of it as you get older.

Here are six key lessons for life:

1. Family time is finite—cherish it.
2. Children time is precious—be present.
3. Friend time is limited—prioritize the real friends.
4. Partner time is meaningful—never settle.
5. Coworker time is significant—find energy.
6. Alone time is abundant—love yourself.

It doesn't matter where you're from, how old you are, or whether you're rich or poor—time is a universal truth and struggle. Your entire life will change the moment you confront the mathematical reality of the amount of time you have remaining with the people you love most.

It serves as a hard reset for your life—an emotionally challenging yet necessary intervention that sparks new awareness and priorities.

Conduct your hard reset in a few simple steps:

1. Start by writing down the name of a friend or family member you love deeply but don't see enough.
2. Approximate the number of times per year that you see that person. Write that number down.
3. Next, write down your age and the other person's age.
4. Subtract the older person's age from eighty (an approximation of life expectancy). This is the approximate number of years you have remaining with this person.
5. Multiply the number of times you see that person per year by the number of years you have remaining with that person.

Use the blank template below to populate your responses.

TIME WEALTH HARD RESET

Friend or family member's name: _____

Number of times seen per year: _____

Your age: _____   **Friend or family member's age:** _____

_____   _____

Subtract the older person's age from 80

80
− _____

Years remaining: _____

Number of times seen per year: ✗ _____

◯

Number of times you will see your loved one before the end

With some terrifyingly simple math, you've determined the number of times you will see your loved one before the end. Repeat the exercise for as many loved ones as you see fit. It will serve as your hard reset—the intervention that will spark new awareness and priorities.

Your entire life will change when you realize that energy fuels growth. Give your energy to stress, complaints, and negative people, they will grow. Give your energy to ambitions, gratitude, and positive people, they will grow. Choose wisely.

THE ENERGY CALENDAR

YOUR OUTCOMES IN LIFE will follow your energy.

You achieve the best outcomes in life when you lean into the activities (and people) that *create energy* and lean away from the activities (and people) that *drain energy*. That requires you to first identify the types of activities and people that fall into each category.

The energy calendar exercise helps you do that.

For a full week, at the end of each day, color-code the activities on your calendar according to whether they were:

- Energy-creating—left you feeling energized during or after—mark them green
- Energy-neutral—no impact—mark them yellow
- Energy-draining—left you feeling depleted during or after—mark them red

You can use the blank calendar on the pages that follow for this assessment.

At the end of the week, look at the full calendar and ask yourself these questions:

- What were the common energy-creating (green) activities?
- What were the common energy-draining (red) activities?

With that information in hand, zoom out and think about ways you can slowly start to lean into energy-creating activities and lean away from energy-draining activities.

There are three primary goals:

	MON	TUE
5:00 A.M.		
6:00 A.M.		
7:00 A.M.		
8:00 A.M.		
9:00 A.M.		
10:00 A.M.		
11:00 A.M.		
12:00 P.M.		
1:00 P.M.		
2:00 P.M.		
3:00 P.M.		
4:00 P.M.		
5:00 P.M.		
6:00 P.M.		
7:00 P.M.		

WED	THU	FRI

1. Energy-creating activities should be prioritized and amplified.
2. Neutral activities should be maintained or delegated.
3. Energy-draining activities should be delegated, removed, or adjusted.

First, write down your energy-creating activities, and brainstorm ways you can lean into these activities to amplify their presence in your life.

ENERGY CREATORS	BRAINSTORM

Next, write down your energy-draining activities, and brainstorm ways to adjust or tweak these activities to make them neutral (or energy-creating). Are there ways you can delegate or remove these activities from your life?

ENERGY DRAINERS	BRAINSTORM

With this information, you can slowly start to make changes to reposition your calendar to improve your ratio of energy-creating to energy-draining.

These changes will have a dramatic impact on your life.

THE TWO-LIST EXERCISE

THE TWO-LIST EXERCISE IS derived from a fabled conversation between legendary investor Warren Buffett and Mike Flint, his personal pilot.

Buffett asked Flint to write down all his professional goals. Then he asked him to circle the top few goals from the list. Finally, he asked him to split the items into two lists: the circled priorities and the non-circled items, which he now called the *Avoid at All Costs List*.

The lesson: The most important items had been highlighted; everything else was simply a distraction threatening to derail Flint's progress.

The two-list exercise is an approach to identifying your most important projects, opportunities, and goals so that you can focus your attention on the things that matter (and say no to the rest).

The two-list exercise has three steps:

STEP 1: MAKE A LIST

Create a comprehensive list of your top professional goals and priorities. Repeat this for your top personal goals and priorities.

PROFESSIONAL	PERSONAL

STEP 2: NARROW THE LIST

Reflect on each of the professional and personal lists. Circle the top two or three items from each list. These should be the absolute top priorities in your professional and personal lives, the items that will have the greatest impact on your long-term trajectory.

PROFESSIONAL	PERSONAL
1.	1.
2.	2.
3.	3.

STEP 3: SPLIT THE LISTS

Write out the Priorities on the left side and the Avoid at All Costs List on the right side.

PROFESSIONAL

PRIORITIES	AVOID AT ALL COSTS
1.	
2.	
3.	

PERSONAL

PRIORITIES	AVOID AT ALL COSTS
1.	
2.	
3.	

Consider this your first line of defense: When a new opportunity arises, refer to your two-list exercise and make a quick assessment of whether it falls into the category of one of your priorities (or if it should be avoided at all costs).

THE EISENHOWER MATRIX

THE EISENHOWER MATRIX IS a productivity tool formulated by author Stephen Covey in his bestselling book *The 7 Habits of Highly Effective People* that forces you to differentiate between the urgent and the important to prioritize and manage your time more effectively.

Urgent tasks require prompt attention. Important tasks advance your long-term values or goals.

While the two-list exercise helps you narrow your attention on a macro level, the Eisenhower Matrix is designed to harness your attention on a micro, daily level.

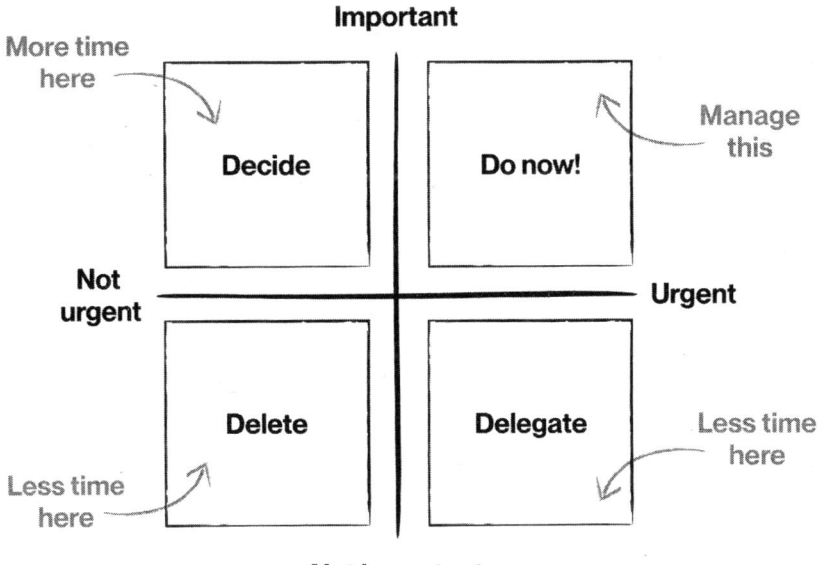

The two-by-two matrix requires you to categorize your tasks into one of four quadrants:

- Important and urgent: These are tasks that require immediate, focused attention but also contribute to your long-term mission or goals.
- Important and not urgent: These tasks are your compounders—they build long-term value in your life.
- Not important and urgent: These tasks are the *Beware* category—they can drain time and energy without contributing to your long-term goals or vision.
- Not important and not urgent: These are the time-wasting tasks and activities that drain your energy and sap your productivity.

The Eisenhower Matrix creates a visual awareness of the types of tasks on which you are spending your time. This awareness allows you to adjust course as necessary to spend most of your time on the important, long-term projects and opportunities.

For one week, write your to-do list items into the following matrix:

EISENHOWER MATRIX

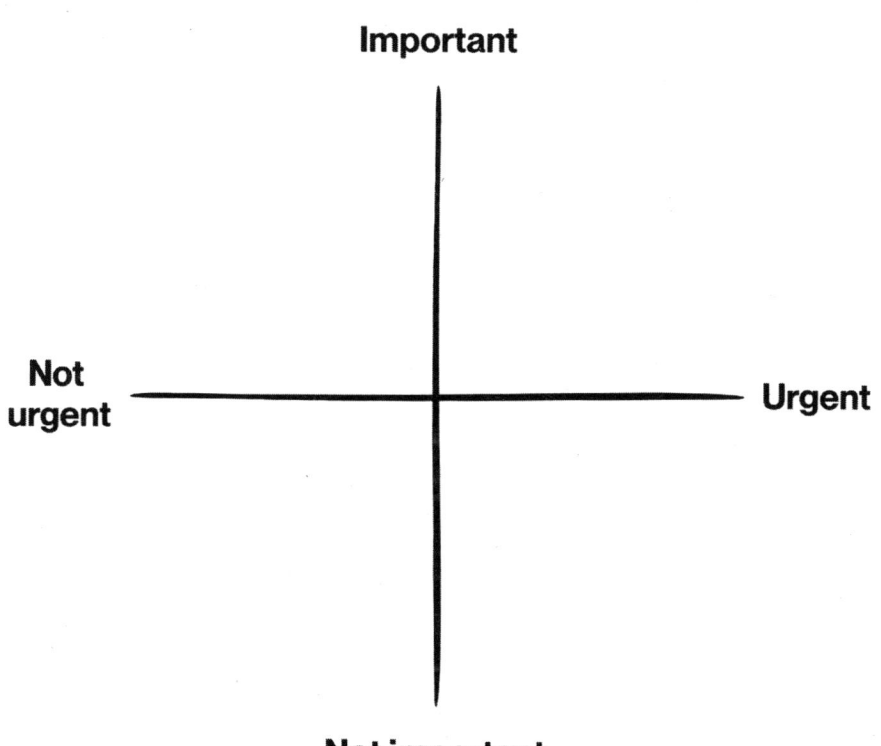

At the end of the week, look at your filled-in matrix and ask two questions:

1. Which quadrant is most densely populated with to-do items?

_____
_____
_____
_____

2. Which quadrant consumed most of your professional hours and headspace?

_____
_____
_____
_____

The goal is to spend most of your time and energy in the top-left quadrant, on the important, not urgent tasks.

Based on these responses, you have a clear sense of what you need to do to improve your mix of activities and time:

- If the top right was heavy, you need to work on getting out in front of important tasks before they become urgent.
- If the bottom right was heavy, you need to work on delegating

these unimportant tasks to someone for whom they will be important.
- If the bottom left was heavy, you need to work on deleting some of these unimportant, low-urgency tasks from your life.

If you identify your trouble areas and make steady, incremental improvements, you'll find your time unlocked for new growth on the other side.

Social Wealth

SOCIAL WEALTH IS BUILT upon three core pillars:

- *Depth:* Connection to a small circle of people with deep, meaningful bonds
- *Breadth:* Connection to a larger circle of people for support and belonging beyond the self, either through individual relationships or through community, religious, spiritual, or cultural infrastructure
- *Earned status:* The lasting respect, admiration, and trust of your peers that you receive on the basis of earned, not acquired, status symbols

In this section, you'll be guided through two exercises to build Social Wealth:

1. The Front-Row People Visualization
2. The Relationship Map

These systems are supported by clear research and battle-tested through my own personal experience. This isn't one-size-fits-all, and you shouldn't feel compelled to complete both; browse through and select those that feel most relevant and useful to you.

Cherish Your Front-Row People

Close your eyes. Imagine you're at your funeral.
People are walking in, crying, hugging each other.
Everyone sits down. Who's in the front row? Those are
the people that really matter. Your Front-Row People.
Find them. Cherish them. Be one to someone else.

THE FRONT-ROW PEOPLE VISUALIZATION

CLOSE YOUR EYES AND take a deep breath. Imagine you're at your funeral. People are walking in, crying, hugging one another. Everyone sits down.

Who is sitting in the front row?

These people—your Front-Row People—are the ones who truly matter.

Let's reflect on a few questions:

Who are the people sitting in the front row at your funeral?

_____
_____
_____
_____
_____

What are you doing to cherish the people who hold those special seats in your world?

_____
_____
_____
_____
_____

How are you letting those people know what they mean to you?

_____
_____
_____
_____

Are you prioritizing time with them or letting it float by and disappear?

_____
_____
_____
_____

What are you doing to be a Front-Row Person to someone else?

_____
_____
_____
_____

Conventional wisdom says one should focus on the journey, not the destination. I disagree. Focus on the *people*. When you surround yourself with inspiring people, the journeys become more beautiful, and the destinations become more brilliant.

It's impossible to sit where you are and plan the perfect journey. Focus on the company—the people you want to travel with—and the journey will reveal itself in due time. Nothing bad has ever come from surrounding oneself with inspiring, genuine, kind, positive-sum individuals.

Find your Front-Row People. Cherish them. Be one to someone else.

THE RELATIONSHIP MAP

THE RELATIONSHIP MAP IS a simple exercise to assess your current social baseline and areas for focus and improvement. It is an adaptation of an exercise proposed in *The Good Life* by coauthors Robert Waldinger and Marc Schulz.

To create your relationship map, follow these three steps:

STEP 1: LIST CORE RELATIONSHIPS

In the space below, list the names of your core social relationships that occupy your life. This may include family, friends, partners, coworkers, and more.

_____
_____
_____
_____
_____
_____
_____
_____
_____
_____
_____
_____
_____
_____

_____
_____
_____
_____
_____
_____

STEP 2: ASSESS CORE RELATIONSHIPS

Assess each relationship across two metrics:

1. **Is the relationship supportive, demeaning, or ambivalent?**

    - A supportive relationship is one where there is mutual understanding of care, love, respect, and comfort.
    - A demeaning relationship is characterized by an absence of supportive qualities.
    - An ambivalent relationship is inconsistent; it has elements of both supportive and demeaning at different times.

2. **Is the relationship interaction frequent or infrequent?**

Next to each person's name, write the quality and frequency of the relationship.

NAME	QUALITY	FREQUENCY

STEP 3: MAP RELATIONSHIPS AND DETERMINE ZONES

Place these core relationships on the blank two-by-two matrix below.

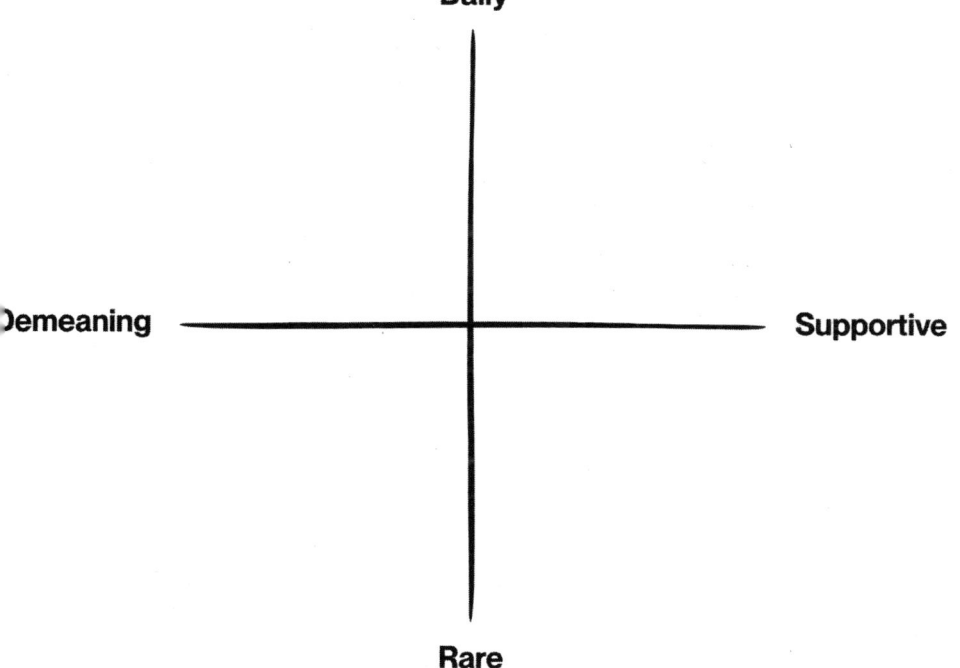

There are four relationship zones to be aware of:

- Green Zone relationships are supportive and frequent. They should be prioritized.
- Opportunity Zone relationships are supportive and infrequent. They should be focused on to increase the frequency.
- Danger Zone relationships are ambivalent and frequent. They should be managed to reduce frequency or improve quality.
- Red Zone relationships are demeaning and frequent. They should be managed or removed.

What are your key learnings from the exercise? What changes do you intend to make based on these learnings?

_____
_____
_____
_____
_____
_____
_____
_____
_____
_____
_____
_____
_____
_____

THE 5 TYPES OF WEALTH LIFE PLANNER

Mental Wealth

MENTAL WEALTH IS BUILT upon three core pillars:

- *Purpose:* The clarity of defining your unique vision and focus that creates meaning and aligns short- and long-term decision-making; the unwillingness to live someone else's life
- *Growth:* The hunger to progress and change, driven by an understanding of the dynamic potential of your intelligence, ability, and character
- *Space:* The creation of stillness and solitude to think, reset, wrestle with questions, and recharge; the ability and willingness to listen to your inner voice

In this section, you'll be guided through three exercises to build Mental Wealth:

1. Finding Your *Ikigai*
2. The Pursuit Map
3. The 1-1-1 Method

These systems are supported by clear research and battle-tested through my own personal experience. This isn't one-size-fits-all, and you shouldn't feel compelled to complete every single one of them; browse through and select those that feel most relevant and useful to you.

FINDING YOUR *IKIGAI*

THE LEGENDARY CENTENARIANS OF Okinawa, Japan, use the concept of *ikigai* to define their life purpose. You can use the concept with a simple exercise to begin to explore yours as well.

Your *ikigai*—your life purpose—sits at the center of three overlapping circles:

1. *What you love:* The activities that are life-giving to you
2. *What you are good at:* The activities that feel effortless
3. *What the "world" needs:* The activities that your current "world" (family, community, region, country, or world) needs from you

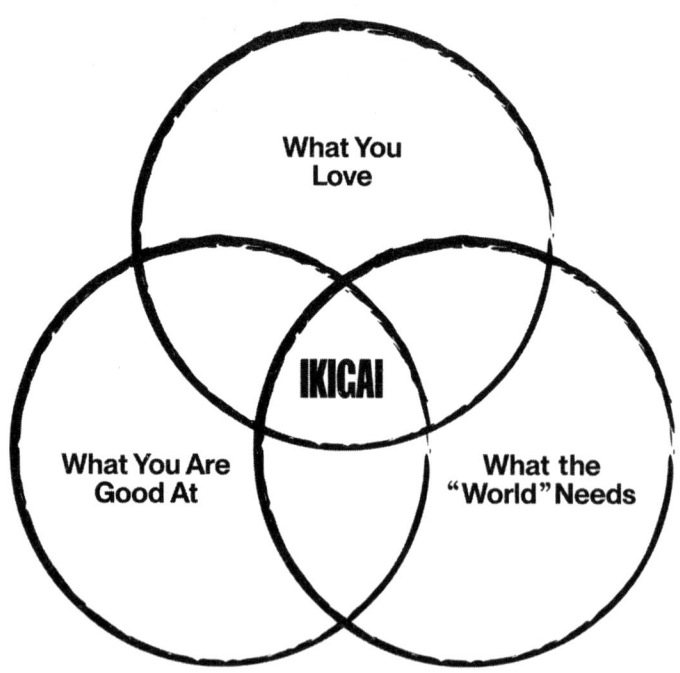

To begin to uncover your *ikigai,* follow these four simple steps:

STEP 1: WHAT YOU LOVE

What activities or responsibilities create joy in your life? What were you doing in the moments when you felt the most natural happiness?

Make a list of the activities that are life-giving. Reflect on what makes them life-giving for you.

_____
_____
_____
_____

STEP 2: WHAT YOU ARE GOOD AT

What feels effortless to you that may be difficult for others? Where do your natural and acquired skills stand out? What do other people seem to recognize as your attributes or skills?

Make a list of the activities that you have unique competency in.

_____
_____
_____
_____

STEP 3: WHAT THE "WORLD" NEEDS

What activities does your world need from you in this season of life?

How you define your world will vary across the seasons. Your world may be defined narrowly by the inner circle of yourself and your family at certain points, by the broader circle of your community at others, and by the broadest circle of the actual world.

In the most common arc, the definition of *world* starts out narrow, grows wider over time, and then ends narrow. It may begin focused on the self and family in the earlier years, expand to focus on the community and grander scale in the middle years, and then go back to the self and family in the later years.

When you have fulfilled the needs of your current world, you feel free to expand that definition on to the next level.

Define your current world, and make a list of the activities that it needs from you.

_____
_____
_____
_____
_____
_____
_____
_____
_____
_____
_____
_____

STEP 4: REFLECT

What is the overlap of the three lists? What activities seem to be coming up across each?

Reflect on the overlap that will provide more clarity on your higher-order life purpose.

_____
_____
_____
_____
_____
_____
_____
_____
_____
_____
_____

Remember that your purpose does not need to be connected to your profession. Work through the exercise and you'll be well on your way to harnessing the power of *ikigai,* just as the Okinawans have.

THE PURSUIT MAP

Your time here is finite, so choosing the pursuits—personal and professional—that deliver the greatest returns on that time is essential.

The pursuit map exercise is a simple approach to identifying the pursuits that are most likely to bring joy and significant rewards into your life.

To create your pursuit map, follow these three steps:

STEP 1: CREATE YOUR MAP

The pursuit map is a blank two-by-two matrix with competency level (from low to high competency) on the x-axis and energy (from energy-draining to energy-creating) on the y-axis.

The terms are defined as follows:

- *High competency:* A pursuit at which you are skilled; these activities feel effortless
- *Low competency:* A pursuit at which you are a novice; these activities feel challenging
- *Energy-creating:* A pursuit that creates energy in your life; these activities leave you feeling energized—they fill your cup
- *Energy-draining:* A pursuit that drains energy from your life; these activities leave you feeling drained—they empty your cup

List and assess your *current pursuits* across these two metrics. Note that for the purposes of this exercise, pursuits can be broadly defined (for example, strategy consulting) or specific (for example, market research).

CURRENT PURSUIT	COMPETENCY	ENERGY

List any *prospective pursuits* you may be interested in. Assume low competency for these prospective pursuits and gather information to assess your energy through conversations with people in these pursuits or small experiments.

PROSPECTIVE PURSUIT	COMPETENCY	ENERGY
	Low	
	Low	
	Low	
	Low	

	Low	
	Low	
	Low	
	Low	
	Low	
	Low	

Place the current and prospective pursuits on the blank pursuit map.

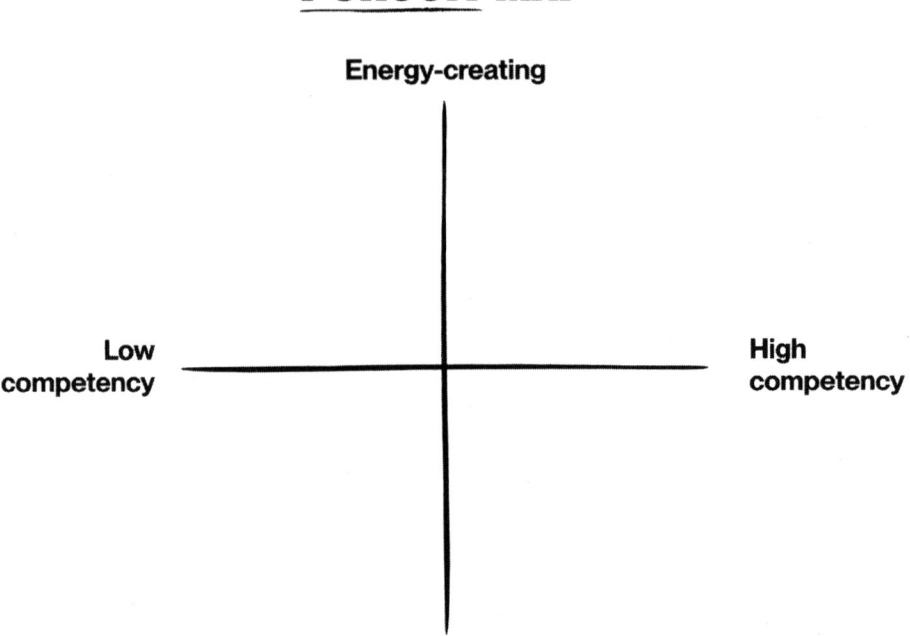

STEP 2: IDENTIFY YOUR ZONES

There are three pursuit zones to be aware of:

- *Zone of Genius:* High competency and energy-creating. A phrase coined by author Gay Hendricks, the Zone of Genius is where you ideally spend most of your time, both personally and professionally.
- *Zone of Danger:* High competency and energy-draining. This is a trap, because you may be given positive feedback and get stuck operating here.
- *Zone of Hobby:* Low competency and energy-creating. It's okay for certain pursuits to remain here!

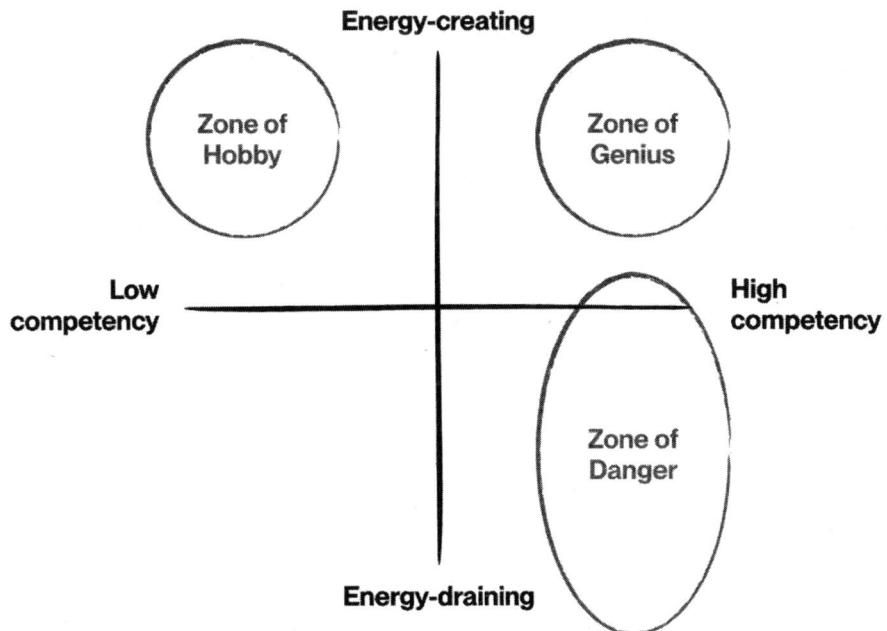

What are the key pursuits that fall into each zone?

GENIUS	DANGER	HOBBY

STEP 3: ALIGN YOUR TIME

Four question prompts to reflect on to complete this exercise:

How can you spend more time in your Zone of Genius?

___
___
___
___
___
___
___
___
___
___

How can you slowly minimize the amount of time you spend in your Zone of Danger?

_____
_____
_____
_____
_____
_____
_____
_____
_____
_____

How can you keep a few things in your Zone of Hobby? What activities are you embracing in this zone?

_____
_____
_____
_____
_____
_____
_____
_____
_____
_____

How can you eliminate the time spent in your dead zone (low competency, energy-draining)?

_____
_____
_____
_____
_____
_____
_____
_____
_____
_____

Choosing the right pursuits is a direct path to a more purpose-filled, fulfilling, productive, and successful life. Learn to follow your energy and you won't be led astray. Conduct the pursuit map exercise and slowly start to work toward a world where your time is invested in the pursuits that provide the greatest rewards.

THE 1-1-1 METHOD

Journaling is an extremely powerful tool for creating space and improving mental health.

Unfortunately, journaling is a habit that eludes most people, often because our impression of the optimal version of journaling gets in the way of developing a realistic, beneficial practice.

The truth: Journaling does not need to be an elaborate, drawn-out experience. Even five minutes of daily journaling can have a profound impact on your mental health.

To build a journaling habit that works in the context of a busy reality, I developed a dead-simple solution: the 1-1-1 Method.

Every single evening, at the end of your day, write down three points:

- One win from the day
- One point of stress, tension, or anxiety
- One point of gratitude

One win allows you to appreciate your progress. One point of stress allows you to get the topic off your mind. One point of gratitude allows you to reflect on the most important things in your life.

The entire process takes about five minutes each evening. It's a simple practice with immediate positive benefits across your life.

To get started, use the space that follows to conduct your 1-1-1 journaling for the week ahead.

DAY 1

DATE: _____

ONE WIN: _____

ONE STRESS: _____

ONE GRATITUDE: _____

DAY 2

DATE: _____

ONE WIN: _____

ONE STRESS: _____

ONE GRATITUDE: _____

DAY 3

DATE: _____

ONE WIN: _____

ONE STRESS: _____

ONE GRATITUDE: _____

DAY 4

DATE: _____

ONE WIN: _____

ONE STRESS: _____

ONE GRATITUDE: _____

DAY 5

DATE: _____

ONE WIN: _____

ONE STRESS: _____

ONE GRATITUDE: _____

DAY 6

DATE: _____

ONE WIN: _____

ONE STRESS: _____

ONE GRATITUDE: _____

DAY 7

DATE: _____

ONE WIN: _____

ONE STRESS: _____

ONE GRATITUDE: _____

Physical Wealth

PHYSICAL WEALTH IS BUILT upon three core pillars:

- *Movement:* Daily body movement through a combination of cardiovascular exercise and resistance training; activities to promote stability and flexibility
- *Nutrition:* Consumption of primarily whole, unprocessed foods to meet major nutrient needs, supplementing as necessary to meet any micronutrient needs
- *Recovery:* High-quality, consistent sleep performance and other recovery-promoting activities

In this section, you'll be guided through two exercises to build Physical Wealth:

1. The Eightieth Birthday Visualization
2. The Morning Routine

These systems are supported by clear research and battle-tested through my own personal experience. This isn't one-size-fits-all, and you shouldn't feel compelled to complete both; browse through and select those that feel most relevant and useful to you.

If you do not change direction, you may end up where you are heading.

—Lao Tzu

THE EIGHTIETH BIRTHDAY VISUALIZATION

Close your eyes and take a deep breath. Imagine you're at your eightieth birthday celebration. All your favorite people are walking in, cards and flowers in hand, big smiles on their faces.

You're sitting at the main table, enjoying your favorite drink and meal, when the ambient music starts to get louder. It's your favorite song. Your foot starts tapping on the floor underneath the table, right along with the beat. Memories of wonderful moments with the song flood back into your brain. People start to get up and walk to the center of the room.

Everyone is looking over at you.

What happens next?

- Do you get up and start dancing with your loved ones?
- Or are you stuck, forced to enjoy the music from your chair?

The harsh truth is that the answers to those questions were written long before you arrived at your eightieth birthday. Your daily actions along the way determined whether you would be dancing or watching at that party.

Let's reflect on a few questions:

If you continue your current daily actions, will you be dancing or watching at your eightieth birthday party?

_____

_____

What actions do you need to add or adjust in the present to more closely align your future with your ideal vision for it?

What would your eighty-year-old self say to you today?

I once asked an eighty-year-old man what advice he would give to his younger self. He expressed a deep regret for the alcohol-heavy, exercise-light lifestyle he had lived throughout his working life. His advice was simple:

Treat your body like a house you have to live in for another seventy years.

Your body is, quite literally, the house that you're going to live in for the rest of your life. You are in control of the present and future state of your house. With a body, just as with a home, if you take care of it today, it will take care of you for years to come.

Let's make sure you're dancing at your eightieth birthday party.

Your Entire Life Will Change When You Realize That Stress and Anxiety Feed on Idleness

When you take action, you starve them of the oxygen they need to survive. The answer is found in the action.

When you arise in the morning, think of what a precious privilege it is to be alive—to breathe, to think, to enjoy, to love.

—Marcus Aurelius

THE MORNING ROUTINE

THE FIRST HOUR OF your morning sets the tone for the entire day ahead. Thoughtful movement and nutrition during that window will make you feel more energized, focused, and productive and provide a sense of structure and stability in an otherwise unpredictable world.

There are five principles to an effective morning routine. This exercise will help you understand and create your own implementation plan for each principle.

PRINCIPLE 1: WAKE UP

Consistent wake times are essential to high functioning. Aim to create a set wake time that is roughly consistent across weekdays and weekends.

Your Implementation Plan: I will wake up at _____ on weekdays and _____ on weekends.

Notes:
_____
_____
_____

PRINCIPLE 2: HYDRATE

Most of us are chronically dehydrated. This affects all areas of health. Morning hydration kick-starts your metabolism, improves memory, and boosts energy.

Your Implementation Plan: I will drink _____ ounces of water upon rising.

Notes:

_____
_____
_____

PRINCIPLE 3: MOVE

Moving your body to start your day is a great way to wake yourself up and prime yourself for whatever activity comes first. I like to use my 5-5-5-30 routine to start my morning: five push-ups, five squats, five lunges, and a thirty-second plank. It takes a couple of minutes and gives me an immediate jolt of energy while my coffee is brewing.

Your Implementation Plan: I will do _____ movement when I get out of bed to get my body ready for the day.

Notes:

_____
_____
_____

PRINCIPLE 4: GET OUTSIDE

Exposure to natural light in the morning increases your focus, improves your mood via increased serotonin production, and serves as a natural source of vitamin D. If nature allows it (temperature, sunrise time), try to get outside for a few minutes to start your day.

Your Implementation Plan: I will walk outside for _____ minutes to start my day.

Notes:

_____
_____
_____

PRINCIPLE 5: FOCUS

If your goal is to create meaningful progress, you must work like a lion. Sprint when inspired. Rest. Repeat. This means starting your day with focus on your priority tasks.

Your Implementation Plan: I will complete focus work on my priority tasks for _____ minutes.

Notes:

_____
_____
_____

PUTTING IT ALL TOGETHER

HERE IS YOUR NEW IDEAL MORNING ROUTINE:

1. Wake Up: I will wake up at _____ on weekdays and _____ on weekends.
2. Hydrate: I will drink _____ ounces of water upon rising.
3. Move: I will do _____ movement when I get out of bed to get my body ready for the day.
4. Get Outside: I will walk outside for _____ minutes to start my day.
5. Focus: I will complete focus work on my priority tasks for _____ minutes.

The best routine is the one that actually helps you get the important things done. Your routine should *serve your life,* not *own it.*

Accordingly, it's important to recognize that you won't always be able to nail this entire routine. If this is your A-level routine, it may benefit you to have a B and C level to fall back on.

To implement this idea, ask yourself the following questions:

What are the habits or actions that get you into a primed state for the day ahead?

_____
_____
_____

Which of those are necessary versus nice to have?

_____
_____
_____

What's the most simplified version if you had to get it done in five minutes or were traveling and in an unfamiliar environment?

_____
_____
_____

Using your responses, create your own version of a B- and C-level morning routine.

My B-Level Routine:

_____
_____

My C-Level Routine:

_____

_____

If you incorporate your own version of these five core principles and develop your A, B, and C levels, you'll be well on your way to building a morning routine that serves your life and enables you to get the important things done.

Financial Wealth

FINANCIAL WEALTH IS BUILT upon three core pillars:

- *Income generation:* Create stable, growing income through primary employment, secondary employment, and passive streams
- *Expense management:* Manage expenses so that they are reliably below your income level and grow at a slower rate
- *Long-term investment:* Invest the difference between your income and expenses in long-term, efficient, low-cost assets that compound effectively

In this section, you'll be guided through one exercise to build Financial Wealth:

1. The Enough Life Visualization

This system is essential. Everyone should complete it.

A gold medal is a wonderful thing, but if you're not enough without it, you'll never be enough with it.

—Irv Blitzer (played by John Candy in *Cool Runnings*)

THE ENOUGH LIFE VISUALIZATION

THERE'S A BEAUTIFUL STORY I love about a banker and a fisherman.

A wealthy banker goes on vacation to a tropical fishing village. As he walks along the docks one afternoon, he comes upon a small, run-down fishing boat with several large fish on its deck.

"How long did it take you to catch those fish?" he asks.

The fisherman looks up from his work and smiles at his new visitor. "Only a little while."

The banker is taken aback by this response. He likes the fisherman and wants to help. "Why don't you fish for longer so you can catch more fish?"

The fisherman shrugs and explains to his new friend that he has all he needs. "Each day, I sleep late, fish a little, and spend time with my children and beautiful wife. In the evening, I go into town, drink wine, play the guitar, and sing and laugh with my friends."

The banker is puzzled. He wants to help his new friend, who, in his opinion, is clearly confused. The banker has helped many businesses and has an MBA and other fancy credentials to his name, so he lays out a plan for the fisherman:

"First, you spend more time fishing so you can catch and sell more fish. You use the proceeds to buy a bigger boat, which allows you to catch and sell even more fish. Then you buy a fleet of boats. You hire a team. Vertically integrate! As the CEO of a large, growing enterprise, you could move to the big city. You would take your company public and make millions!"

The fisherman looks confused, but smiles. "And then what?" he asks.

The banker laughs at the silly question. "Well, then you could retire to a quiet town! You could sleep late, fish a little, and spend time with your children and beautiful wife. In the evening, you could go into town, drink wine, play the guitar, and sing and laugh with your friends."

The fisherman smiles broadly, thanks his new friend for the advice, and wanders off slowly in the warm afternoon sun.

The popular interpretation of this parable is that the banker is wrong and the fisherman is right. My own interpretation is that this story isn't about the fisherman being right and the banker being wrong—it's about identifying what success and purpose look like to you and building a life that meets that definition.

It's about defining what *enough* means to you.

The goal of this visualization is to create a clear image of your *Enough Life*. And importantly, the Enough Life doesn't have to be simple or spartan; it can be as ambitious or lavish as you see fit.

The point is that it is *your* Enough Life—not someone else's, not influenced by social or cultural pressures, not prone to the subconscious escalation of lifestyle creep. By defining it, by writing it down and keeping it top of mind, you force it into the conscious mind. This doesn't perfectly halt the natural upward movement, but it does convert an irrational, subconscious movement into a rational, conscious one.

EXERCISE: YOUR ENOUGH LIFE

To create your image, reflect on the following question prompts (and discuss them with your partner if you have one):

Where do you live? Are you living in a house, apartment, or something else? What specific characteristics do you love about the place where you live?

_____
_____
_____
_____
_____

Do you spend all your time in one place or live in different places?

_____
_____
_____
_____
_____

With whom do you live? Are you close to family or far away?

_____
_____
_____
_____
_____

What are you doing on an average Tuesday? What are you spending your time on? What are you working on? What are you thinking about?

_____
_____
_____
_____

What material things do you have? What are the objects or possessions that truly bring joy to your life?

_____
_____
_____
_____

What do you have the flexibility to spend money on freely?

_____
_____
_____
_____

What does your financial profile look like? What amount of money enables that life? How much cushion do you have in your finances?

_____
_____
_____
_____

What are you earning, saving, and investing each month? How much of a safety net do you have?

_____
_____
_____
_____

Once you have a clear, vivid image of your Enough Life, you can use it as a tool for planning:

- What is the gap from your present reality to that future reality?
- What are the key steps and actions necessary to bridge that gap?

The Enough Life exercise is one that can be completed every few years. The beauty of living your Enough Life is waiting—define it, imagine it, then start working to build it.

The 5 Types of Wealth Decision Template

As you encounter the bigger inflection points and decisions on your journey, use the following template to assess and reflect on the impact they will have on all five types of wealth.

Key Decision: _____

	IMPACT (+/-)	REFLECTION NOTES
Time Wealth		
Social Wealth		
Mental Wealth		
Physical Wealth		
Financial Wealth		

With this template in hand, you are well equipped to make better decisions and take the right actions as you progress toward your vision for the future.

	IMPACT +/-/neutral	REFLECTION
TIME		
SOCIAL		
MENTAL		
PHYSICAL		
FINANCIAL		

Conclusion

I AM LIVING MY dream life because I embraced a better way. Now it's time for you to do the same.

Measure, make decisions, and design your new life around these five types of wealth:

- Time Wealth
- Social Wealth
- Mental Wealth
- Physical Wealth
- Financial Wealth

Measure your life across all the pillars of a happy, fulfilling existence. Establish your baseline Wealth Score, then come back to it each year to assess your progress and areas of opportunity.

Make decisions that consider all five types of wealth. Rather than narrowly focusing on Financial Wealth, evaluate a decision based on its impact on all five types of wealth. The most important decisions are best made with the full spectrum of your life in mind.

Design your dream life within and across the seasons to come.

CONCLUSION

Use this new model for proactive life design that considers your changing priorities and enables you to focus on specific individual battles without sacrificing your victory in the longer-term war. Navigate life's uncertainty with clarity as you evaluate the trade-offs you are willing and unwilling to make to build the life you want.

In the letter at the beginning of this *Life Planner*, I offered the following:

Awareness is nothing without action.

Well, here you are: You have the information. You have the tools. Only one thing remains. And fortunately, it's entirely within your control.

Three, two, one . . . Action.